AFTER THE PLANNERS

ROBERT GOODMAN

PENGUIN BOOKS

To Sarah and Julia
AND ALL THOSE BRAVE PEOPLE
WHO WON'T PUT UP WITH IT

Penguin Books Ltd, Harmondsworth,
Middlesex, England
Penguin Books Australia Ltd, Ringwood,
Victoria, Australia
First published in the U.S.A. by Simon & Schuster
and in Great Britain by Pelican Books 1972

Copyright © Robert Goodman, 1972

Made and printed in Great Britain by
Compton Printing Ltd, Aylesbury

CONTENTS

of counter-revolution—concepts of Robert Venturi and
Edward T. Hall.

The conservative bias of city-planning reforms. Making it legal—zoning and city-planning commissions.
Liberal programs for integration through zoning and
education foster racism. Enter the technocrats and
pseudo-science—Rexford Tugwell makes a classic case.
Daniel P. Moynihan and the urban medicine men.

Advocacy planning, pluralism and capitalism—the contradictions. Community-socialism, "just outputs" and
cultural revolution. Revolutionary demands and guerrilla architecture. Some lessons from "primitive" cultures. New forms and a new commitment.

ACKNOWLEDGMENTS

OFTEN AGREEING with the content of my arguments, some readers of the manuscript of this book have been concerned about the style of my presentation. They would have hoped for a less "bitter" analysis. Perhaps for another subject and another time in history, a gentler form would have been in order. But if this book reveals my contempt for the inequity and injustice that traditional planning helps promote in this country, then let that rage stand at least to symbolize that some of us will not be content to allow it to continue. If some part of why that contempt exists and what we can do about it can be felt by the reader, then perhaps in some way this writing will move us closer to a time when our acts turn from anger and frustration to a life of living in peace with one another.

In writing this book I have had help from many people. Most especially for reviewing the critical ideas, providing new insights and suggesting material, I thank my good friend Yanni Pyriotis. To make possible the ponderous task of gathering material on numerous planning proposals, projects and theories of urban experts, I had the intelligent help of Joan Fleischnick, Hannah Kaltman, Nathan Rome and Suzanne Weinberg. For their ideas, editorial help and encouragement I owe more than gratitude to Diane Berman, Rosalind Krauss, Anita Landa, Rhea Wilson, and Gillie Terry. Pamela Bedrosian, Nancy Jones and Ellen Berman I really don't know how to thank—they've put up with a multitude of changes and rewrites in their typing work; I ask

ACKNOWLEDGMENTS

their forgiveness. For their assistance in financing part of this study I express my gratitude to the Community Projects Laboratory of the Architecture Department at the Massachusetts Institute of Technology. Thanks, if any, to my father and mother, without whose help the world would have been spared one more book, will have to be accorded by the reader. My apologies and gratitude to all those people whose help was crucial and whose names I haven't mentioned. Finally, like everyone else, I thank you all, but I take responsibility for what follows.

ROBERT GOODMAN

Cambridge, Massachusetts

INTRODUCTION TO
THE BRITISH EDITION

THE PUBLICATION of *After the Planners* in the United Kingdom is timely when planning plays an increasingly important role in government and business. This book is the result of Robert Goodman's experience as an 'advocate planner' attempting to compensate for the lack of expertise of poor urban communities countering insensitive and often unjust 'planned' change in American cities. Through his experience as an advocate for the poor, Goodman came to realize that it was not merely lack of expertise which lay at the roots of such communities' problems, but the political, economic and cultural context of American society. Since many of the tendencies, inconsistencies and contradictions which Goodman analyses are also apparent in our own society, and in our planning apparatus, his arguments give us many insights into our own situation.

As Goodman himself points out in his Introduction, he was never a part of either the hippy underground culture nor a radical in the sense that he had a political analysis of his situation to fall back on. His experience as a 'counter-professional' and his analysis of the reasons why expertise, science and objective analysis have failed to come to grips with the explosion of urban problems in post-war America arose from his personal idealism. He reacted against what he calls 'an insistent pattern of arrogant and repressive programmes' carried out by planners, politicians and corporate interests. Like many other young people brought up in the over-developed society, his original stand has led him farther into a rejection of the life-styles of consumption and bureaucratic control that Herbert Marcuse has defined as the 'one-dimensional society'. Above all, he is one of those seeking a new politics, a new ideology for a morally acceptable social change.

Goodman speaks not only in the voice of young Americans, but what he has to say describes the contradictions and dilemmas of the developed western world. His position can be compared with that put forward in the manifesto of a group of planners and architects from Europe and Latin America, who came together in a planning school in London in 1970. They too quote from an American in describing their own intellectual development.

My own social and intellectual background is that of middle-class North America . . . I was . . . 'on the Left, where the heart is'. . . However I was fundamentally irresponsible; I was an intellectual schizophrenic; I kept my political opinion and my intellectual and professional work apart, accepting scientific theories more or less as they were handed to me and forming my political opinions largely in response to feeling and isolated facts. Like many of my colleagues I was a liberal. To learn to do research in the social sciences worthy of the name, to become socially and politically more responsible, and to dare to tell people . . . what political economy of growth might serve them, I had to free myself from the liberal maxim, according to which only political neutrality permits scientific objectivity, pseudo-scientific scientism and political reaction. I had to learn that *social* science must be *political* science.*

*Capitalism and Underdevelopment in Latin America, A. G. Franks, quoted in An Alternative Programme for Study, Arias, Diaz, von Gavel, Saccheri; Architectural Association, 1970.

For these students too, radicalism grew out of direct experience of planning and architectural practice in their own countries. What unites each of these small groups of disaffected professionals and students is an understanding that the result of planning at national, regional or city-wide levels is the support or *rationalization* of the status quo, in situations where fundamental changes are necessary. If planning is not about the redistribution of the resources or the benefits of an unequal society, then it can only be an instrument of bureaucratic conservatism. The political role of planning is clearly demonstrated by an analysis of the context for planning, planning practice, and the structure of the planning profession such as Robert Goodman achieves in this book.

His first concern is with the close identification of interests which has developed between politicians and industry in the United States, and with the planners' crucial role as facilitators in a grossly manipulated system. Yet there are certain obvious weaknesses in this system which are apparent not only to professionals and politicians, but also to the public they serve. There is an increasing distance between workers and those unions and managements who take decisions on their behalf; between residents in the city, particularly if they are poor, and those who represent and govern them; between the claims of politicians and industrialists that people have never had it so good, and the actual experience of those who have never had it in any material sense, and who are progressively alienated from any responsibility for their lives at work and in their communities. Goodman's second concern arises directly out of this. He believes that since the problems of present American urban society are inherent in its structure, then the efforts of reformers are doomed to failure. You cannot, he argues, graft pluralist mechanisms, such as Advocacy

Planning, onto existing relationships to solve problems of democratic control if the existing relationships are so unbalanced as to discount the effect of the proposed reform. In order to gain acceptance, any reform is made to fit the status quo and as a result it is disarmed as an effective mechanism for change.

Faced with this situation, planners will tend to react in a number of ways. Many will undoubtedly accept the status quo as the natural state of affairs, and will go on with their own activities unquestioningly. For them planning will always occur within the boundaries of what is politically, administratively, or professionally possible. To that extent they are 'yes-men' whose opinions and skills can be relied upon to reinforce rather than undermine the society, whatever its nature. A second tendency, towards reformism, will be demonstrated by those planners who, whilst not questioning the underlying relationships in the society, will nevertheless press through their work for a more equal distribution of rights or benefits. Pointing to the exclusion of certain classes or groups of people from knowledge of, or participation in, the planning process, they will offer to put their professional skills to work in representing and interpreting the interests of the groups concerned. Unfortunately, while acting as an advocate for the poor may prove to be very rewarding for the professional, it effectively minimizes the necessity for any of the rules of the game being changed so as to include the poor themselves.

A third tendency will be manifested by those who work towards simplistic or utopian solutions to the problems confronting them. Dismayed by the complexities of the societies they are asked to plan, utopians will find an intellectual or emotional 'cop-out'. For example, the idea that urban designers can ignore the realities of cultural and economic relationships and change the society through the nature of the environments they design, one of the fundamental tenets of the modern movement in architecture, is clearly wishing away any number of hard realities. It is also an élitist philosophy, for once the planner sees himself working towards his own solution for the environment as an independent variable, then people and relationships, the dependent variables, are open to manipulation to suit the designer's schema.

In practice these alternatives are rarely self-contained, and any given situation will conjure up from the planners involved a mixture of responses from the current systems of belief. For this reason Robert Goodman puts forward a fourth alternative which he envisages as being much more clear-cut. If the problems of inequality are deeply embedded structural problems in American society, and if planned intervention in that system only serves to reinforce rather than remove the inequalities, then the intervention for change must come from outside the system and it too must be a planned intervention. This time, however, the motive force behind the 'planning' must come from those people who are excluded from the machinery of government and power. Goodman calls for a new professionalism which sees its main purpose as the creation of a cultural revolution in which the first step towards change is the breaking down of class barriers and in which intellectuals and professionals desert their present roles and help create a joint educational experience for layman and professional alike. The practice of the particular professional skill, whether planning, architecture, teaching, law, medicine or whatever, will always be secondary to this first principle. The injustices and inconsistencies of the society must be confronted wherever they occur in everyday life, and lessons must be drawn for future development and action. Goodman's book demonstrates the

13

richness of the field of urban planning in the United States for such lessons.

For the British reader, however, there are a number of further questions to be answered before similar conclusions can be drawn. Firstly, is the relationship between government and industry which Goodman identifies in America of a similar kind in Britian? What is the function of planning in this equation? What is the role of the planning profession, and to what extent does the profession accept its role? Is Goodman's call for a new professionalism of relevance to the British situation? These are complex questions which in many ways require another book parallel to Goodman's to answer properly. Nevertheless in this Introduction the arguments will be put forward that *After the Planners* has important lessons to teach us about the function of planning in a capitalist society, and that in Britain, more than America, the conditions exist for planning to be an efficient mechanism for social control of the Welfare State.

Whereas in the United States, with its Federal Government structure and decentralized city or state power bases, alliances are built up between politicians, their staffs, and the lobbyists for the technostructure, in Britain the stronger government machine with its permanent civil service at national and local levels enables a much better integrated relationship with industry and capital to take place. Since planning in both Britain and the USA is seen in terms of an essentially governmental or corporate intervention in a given field of activity, then the development of differing processes of government in the two countries has brought about differences in the practice of planning. Emphasis should be laid on 'practice', however, because in theory planning has a similar function in any capitalist organization, whether corporation or state. Goodman

14

therefore identifies the function of the planner in the alliance between politician and industry as that of go-between or facilitator in matters affecting urban growth and change. In the British situation his function is slightly different for a number of reasons. The most important is that the majority of British planners, unlike their American counterparts, are direct employees of government on long-term contracts, and not consultants or employees retained for the duration of a particular programme or government. Thus the British planner is as subject to political pressure from above, but less likely to get personally involved in the debates and power groupings affecting the communities for which he plans. He can therefore maintain an apparent neutrality which is reinforced by his allegiance to stronger professional institutions than those of the United States. He is also more likely to do what he is told by his immediate political masters because he has nowhere else to work. In Britain then, the role of the planner is directly determined by the relationship between government and industry, and the government's other major client groups.

The interdependence between government and business can be seen most clearly in four phases of planning in Britain since the mid-nineteenth century, covering the development of environmental, regional and economic, and social planning. Each phase in the development of a progressively more all-embracing planning machine as part of the government/business technostructure followed closely upon contemporary crises and preoccupations of British capitalism. During the first phase the excesses and brutality of the industrial revolution were found to be an impediment to continuing industrial expansion and economic growth as poor housing, disease and squalor imperilled not only the labour forces on which extractive and manufacturing

industries depended, but also through their close proximity the lives of the middle classes and *nouveaux riches*.
Urban working-class conditions were also causal factors
in crime and social unrest which, remembering the
example of the French Revolution, had to be ameliorated
if a similar upheaval were to be avoided in British
society.

The second phase found Britain exhausted by a major
European war, with a rapidly declining share of world
trade, faced with revolution and unrest in Europe, and
mass unemployment at home. The next phase again
found the country recovering from a major war, while
the fourth phase, which we are now in, finds the country
again confronted by a declining share of world trade,
needing to maintain a competitive stance in world
markets while fighting inflation at home.

TOWN AND COUNTRY PLANNING

Congestion, unbalanced development and underdevelopment have always been features of capitalist industrial
societies, and the attempts by some early nineteenth-
century social reformers to bring to public notice the
conditions of disease and poverty in which the working
classes lived were characteristic of deeply ingrained
middle-class attitudes. Attention was focused not on the
causes of poverty, but on the extent to which the poor
were a burden on the local public purse. It was widely
believed that the administration of the Poor Laws was
too lax since it encouraged shiftlessness and led to
degeneration because it allowed those on relief to live
and have children at the public expense. Reform, when
it came, concentrated on these 'abuses' of the system,
rather than on the new social problems of the industrial-
izing regions. As a result, social investigators and
reformers devoted much time and energy up to the

end of the nineteenth century informing a constantly shocked public of how little previous reforms relieved large bodies of the working classes from actual destitution.

In spite of campaigns to change conditions in factories, mines, housing and the urban environment, it is difficult to know how successful reformers would have been given the prevailing climate of opinion, without a number of circumstances combining to force public attention to the fact that the population was being 'poisoned by its own excrement'. Cholera swept across the country in 1831-2, 1848-9, 1853-4 and again in 1866. Housing conditions, overcrowding and lack of even the most primitive sanitation in the city, were linked by the reformers with the spread of disease, as well as with other forms of 'moral' degradation.

As the industrial cities grew, the separation between the middle classes and working classes became marked. Segregation in the social and economic life of the two communities was duplicated in the development of separate areas of the town for their accommodation. This had the effect of removing those who could afford it from the areas of crime, disease and squalor, and relieving their sensibilities, whilst at the same time leaving the workers in a suitable proximity to the factory belt. Many of the so-called Utopians, like James Buckingham, retained these useful social distinctions in their theories on the Ideal City. Idealistic social reformers often had to link their arguments to practical considerations to gain a hearing, and the most effective argument was that sanitary and housing reform would actually *save money* for the rate-payer in the long run. Poverty, undernourishment, ill-health and overcrowded conditions would sap the spirit and strength from the workers and place a burden on public charity; whereas in a good environment their health and well-being, and

17

hence their productivity, would be ensured. Public
health and working-class housing became an increasingly important preoccupation of the government and
by the 1890s a number of strands in the reform movements – utopian urban design, promotion of public
health, the provision of services, improved working-
class housing, and urban government reform – were
being put together in a series of arguments for proper
town planning as the best means of coordinating the
reform and future growth of urban areas. Prevention
was better than cure, and planning was intended to
prevent similar occurrences in the future by ensuring
proper building standards, and through zoning, the
minimization of industrial nuisance in residential areas.
Planning would benefit the workers and bourgeoisie
resident in the city; the landowners by maintaining the
overall value of developed land through the preservation of 'character' and social standing of particular
neighbourhoods; and the capitalists through the cultiva-
tion of healthy work-forces. The Housing and Town
Planning Acts of 1909 and 1919 were therefore the
culminating points of this first phase, in which health,
housing and planning were linked for the first time in
national legislation.

ECONOMIC PLANNING AND THE REGIONAL PROBLEM

The nineteenth- and early twentieth-century development of modern town planning is important not only for
an understanding of planning practice and the state of
our urban areas today, but also because it has common
roots with other elements of the modern Welfare State.
Between 1918 and 1939, while the principles of town
planning were refined and consolidated, changes were

also taking place in the fields of employment, health and social-welfare policies.

The 1914–18 war had seen the first major government interventions in what had previously been an open-market system. Most important, the government had nationalized the coal, shipping and railway industries for the duration of the war, introduced a new principle – conscription – into the manning of the armed forces, and carried out increasingly extensive planning of manpower and resources to meet the urgent needs for a wide range of war supplies. Demobilization and the falling-off in production at the end of the war created a growing unemployment problem at home, and the need for long-term adjustments to the British economy. Britain's share of world trade had been falling steadily in the years leading up to the war, and dropped by an enormous 20 per cent between 1914 and 1918. The decline was most sharply felt in the traditional industries of coal, cotton and wool, which were the mainstay of the new industrial and urban regions of the nineteenth century. There were dangers in this situation not only from the effects of recession on the national economy, but in the example that the Russian Revolution and the general restlessness of workers all over Europe set for the unemployed and underemployed in tightly packed urban communities in Britain. Industrial disputes occurred with growing frequency and severity, leading to the General Strike in 1926.

The solutions offered in this situation depended upon one crucial decision: the extent to which it was right for government to use the powers of coordination and intervention in the free market it had assumed in wartime to solve the problems of peace. In the immediate post-war years, the demand for a return to normality and 'business as usual' was strong, and the government quickly dismantled much of its emergency machinery. Yet, with

19

growing unemployment and social unrest, new national machinery was set up to coordinate health insurance, pensions, labour and eventually unemployment insurance. In 1934 a new Unemployment Assistance Board saw its functions as being not only to provide assistance to people in need of work, but to promote their welfare through industrial re-training schemes, help in transference to other parts of the country where work was available, and special help for those too old to hope for further regular employment. Although most aspects of social and welfare policy during the twenties and early thirties were concerned with the relief of poverty, the remedies were directed to the relief of symptoms of need, and government intervention left the market free to sort out its own economic problems as best it could.

It was not until the designation of 'Special Areas' and the setting up of the Royal Commission on the Distribution of Industrial Population in 1937 that something approaching Beveridge's call (in 1909) for National Planning as part of the insurance against unemployment was suggested. The Commission was set up to deal specifically with problems of regional economic imbalance and the long-term unemployment problem, and recommended government action to remedy the situation as a counterpart to the contribution the state already made through insurance and aid. It called for a 'reasonable balance of industrial development, so far as possible, throughout the various divisions or regions of Great Britain', the redevelopment of congested areas, and the dispersal of industry. By considering the earlier preoccupations with housing at the same time as unemployment and the distribution of industry, the recommendations became one of the most compelling arguments for town planning, and at the time of the publication of the Commission's Report in 1940, the first of a series of important documents which were to in-

20

fluence post-war planning and reconstruction. It was particularly influential in the development of the New Towns and of government aid to regions with special industrial problems, and represented the first attempt by government at overt industrial planning.

ECONOMIC PLANNING AND THE WELFARE STATE

With the outbreak of the Second World War, almost all new construction and development halted, and the recommendations of the Report on Industrial Population had to be shelved. The powers of coordination which the government assumed, however, achieved much that had been demanded in the thirties and set precedents and patterns for subsequent government action. The foundations were laid for the post-war 'mixed economy', in which, for the first time the activities of the public sector were to influence the direction and success of national economic policies. The direction, coordination and programming of industry and resources during the war was to develop the machinery necessary to institute national economic planning once the war was over.

The country's morale was sustained by the setting up of a number of committees to consider urgent problems of post-war reconstruction and policy. Several of these were to have important bearings on planning in both its traditional and new forms. The Uthwatt Committee on Compensation and Betterment put forward recommendations which paved the way for the 'comprehensive redevelopment' of both war-damaged areas, and of the congested areas referred to by the Barlow Commission. The Scott Committee gave recommendations regarding the Utilization of Land in Rural Areas. Most influential

21

of them all was the Beveridge Committee on Social Insurance and Allied Services. Not only was Beveridge's Report the most influential, but his personal vision was the most all-embracing.

Beveridge summarized this vision, as well as satisfying a need for national goals and incentives, when he put his social security programme in the context of a general programme of social policy to attack five fundamental evils: want, disease, ignorance, squalor and idleness. The last two of these evils clearly pointed to the need for proper planning of industrial distribution and population, as well as economic planning for full employment. Without undue cynicism at Beveridge's expense, the vision was certainly well-timed. As in the period immediately following the first great war, government had to be prepared for post-war recession, unemployment and subsequent social unrest. This was certainly a major concern of a number of the Ministers and Members of Parliament who spoke in the parliamentary debate on the Beveridge Report. Amongst them, Captain Quintin Hogg had no doubts as to the feelings of the men on the battle front:

Some of my Honourable Friends seem to overlook one or two ultimate facts about Social Reform. The first is that if you do not give the people Social Reform, they are going to give you Social Revolution. Let anyone consider the possibility of a series of dangerous industrial strikes, following the present hostilities, and the effects it would have on our industrial recovery. . .*

Beveridge himself saw the value of such government plans for helping each individual citizen to concentrate on his own war effort.

An important underlying assumption of Beveridge's work, which he pursued further after the war, was that policies aimed at full employment were a fundamental

* Parliamentary Proceedings, vol. 386, col. 1918.

prerequisite of his plans for social security. They were also equally important for successive post-war governments in their search for fast economic growth and stability. Planning therefore became concerned with more than its previous commitment to the rationalization of town and country into compatible activities, to the maintenance of standards in health, public services and transport, and to the civic design of towns and cities. It used the opportunities created first through the need to reconstruct war-damaged areas, and later through the redevelopment of outworn centres and Victorian developments, to further the creation of the New Towns and industrial decentralization. It was also concerned with attempts to divert economic growth away from those parts of the country in which it was 'naturally' occurring, to areas of underdevelopment or to those areas where the impetus of the nineteenth century was long spent.

Once again, if planning was to do more than continually respond to the regular crises of unregulated capitalism, it needed to be able to look ahead to the time when fresh problems might emerge. Just as town planners were already drawing up development plans which attempted to coordinate and phase the structural changes occurring in the environment, so the regional and economic planners needed to be able to look ahead to periods of future economic and industrial change in order to prepare for the introduction of new forms of industry and for the re-training of labour forces. Conversely, industry and capital needed the reassurance and security of government planning at national and regional levels as a safety net for the activities of the market place. There in short are the motivations for government and business cooperation in economic planning.

Far from representing an increasing democratic

control over economic developments as is often thought, a number of economists have seen in state planning a necessary corollary of increasing industrial diversification, lengthening production cycles, corporate organization and international spread. The economist Andrew Schonfield argues that in the economic field planning started as a device for the solution of a specific problem – overcoming past neglect of certain industries is one example he gives – and only later became of real relevance to the whole range of economic policy issues. Thus planning becomes a means by which sudden changes in the economic infrastructure, such as those caused through accelerating technological change, can be made less sudden. In other words, planning is an attempt to absorb sudden jolts within the system.

Although such arguments are specifically concerned with economic planning, they are also apposite to the development of town planning and the Welfare State in its different guises and manifestations. These too started as solutions to particular problems and developed into coordinated responses to changing conditions. It is this version of planning, greasing the wheels for industrial and technological change, which concerns Robert Goodman in the early part of his book. When he quotes from *Business Week* (Chapter III, page 127) in showing how the demand for better housing, transportation and medical care are dependent on Federal initiative to open up the problem areas created by the working of the market for new market exploitation, he identifies a problem for all capitalist systems. Government intervention in any field is usually resisted as long as there are few capital risks involved for the market. Thus government may set minimum standards in the field of housing, for example, but does not need to intervene more directly until part of the housing market begins to break down. In England this occurred as early as 1924, when it became necessary for local councils to start building their own working-class dwellings for rent, because it was apparent that the private sector would not finance improved housing at the required standard, and because the job was too large for the charitable institutions. Again, government does not need to enter fields such as industrial location or nationalization and subsidy, unless there are already shortcomings which the market alone cannot overcome, or wider questions such as national security, for which the market is not responsible. In the face of shortcomings in the system, it becomes necessary for government pump-priming to restart the profitability cycle, not only for the good of a single industry or town, but because of the implications for a complex web of inter-relationships if one link breaks down.

THE MOVE TOWARDS SOCIAL PLANNING

The final phase in the development of planning in Britain is more difficult to describe adequately than the others. For one reason, we are in the middle of it, and perhaps it would therefore be more accurate to describe it as a series of tendencies which are developing a new direction for planning. Yet looking at the development of planning so far, from single-issue problem-solving to attempts at across-the-board coordination, it is arguable that the rigid departmentalization of the Welfare State bureaucracy, with its emphasis on the *relief* of poverty, is due to make some form of attempt at social coordination and programming. This would have as its main objective the minimization of the need for relief mechanisms, and the creation of a consumer society in which all members participate through their own un- aided efforts. One would hypothesize that this would

25

take the form of an attempt to plan and coordinate social policy on a wide scale, with an emphasis on identifying future trouble areas for the mobilization of preventative machinery. One would further argue that such social planning will be geared, as previously, to the needs of the technostructure and national security.

The first evidence for the need for such a social planning machine must be drawn from the experience of planning and urban renewal in post-war Britain, during the period when the ideology of the present Welfare State was at its zenith. The early period of urban renewal and redevelopment which occurred from 1948 onwards was necessary, and probably the best that could be achieved under the prevailing circumstances. Unfortunately, the methods and techniques and above all the planning mentality which developed during those years were crucially formative in determining the nature of subsequent urban renewal. The redevelopment of 'obsolete areas' (in planning terminology), and the rehabilitation of the less worn areas of urban Britain were undertaken with an arrogant disregard for human and social consequences.

The older urban areas have come under great pressure as economic and social change, unmitigated by the effect of government planning, has come about. The redistribution and specialization in central area activities; the development of new transportation routes and 'interchanges'; new and expanded facilities for tourism, business and entertainment; programmes of comprehensive public renewal and redevelopment; the commercial enterprises and office complexes; the educational precincts and housing projects: these have all been planned, costed, debated and built. The resulting environmental disasters are only too obvious; the social and economic consequences less so.

These pressures have had a very direct effect on the

26

urban working populations in particular. The poorest inhabitants are moved around, always one step ahead of the developers, like frantic urban nomads. Escape routes to the suburbs or New Towns are blocked by the gatekeepers of the housing- and job-markets, who effectively determine the pace of upward social mobility which the system demands as proof of the individual's worth. Thus lack of skill, cultural bias, or plain apathy force such people and their families to remain in the heart of the city where they accept a situation in which bad education, poor job-prospects and obsolescent housing, linked to growing insecurity, are their future and their past.

Peter Wilmott and Michael Young have described the effects of family and community disruption during the processes of urban renewal; then and subsequently, planners and politicians have taken it for granted that whatever the consequences of their programmes, the blow will be softened by the availability of the Welfare State machinery. This too has proved a myth, as the research of Titmus, Townsend, Abel-Smith, Cullingworth, Greve and many others has shown. It cannot be claimed either that the social and economic disruption caused by urban renewal was unanticipated. It was clearly used, when necessary, to obliterate rather than solve the intractable problems of poverty in the city. In this, too, the British experience exactly parallels that of the United States, although until recently the planners have had a far easier time in Britain. Disruption as a policy was typified in the writing in the early 1960s of Newcastle's City Planning Officer, who is now Chief Planner at the Department of the Environment.

In a huge city, it is a fairly common observation that the dwellers in a slum area are almost a separate race of people with different values, aspirations, and ways of living... One

27

result of slum clearance is that a considerable movement of people takes place over long distances, with devastating effect on the social groupings built up over the years. But, one might argue, this is a good thing when we are dealing with people who have no initiative or civic pride. The task surely is to break up such groupings even though the people seem to be satisfied with their miserable environment and seem to enjoy an extrovert social life in their own locality.*

This advice was given in a textbook written to show the more backward local authorities and planning students how an expert should go about the task of urban renewal in the 1960s. Yet Wilmott and Young's study of the effect of urban renewal on communities in the East End of London had been published in 1957, six years previously, and received wide publicity and comment. In addition, local authority welfare departments and government Social Security offices were receiving a steady stream of the recipients of such 'planned' urban problem-solving, in every town and city where urban renewal was undertaken.

This view of the function of urban renewal still has much currency among professionals and politicians alike, and many urban-renewal schemes now going ahead or planned for the future have a large element of disruption built into them. Nevertheless, it is an extremely inefficient method of planning in the long term. There is pressure building up from within the planning profession and from the public for programmes of complementary social policies to be undertaken along with urban renewal. Although based on a rather narrow conception of what social planning could mean, it is nevertheless an important straw in the wind. The function of urban renewal presupposes an attack upon environmental poverty. So, the argument runs, the comprehensive replanning of wider land-uses and trans-

* Wilfred Burns, *New Towns for Old*, Leonard Hill, 1963.

28

portation, the provision of new facilities such as shops, schools, swimming pools, and playgrounds can be categorized as social inputs to the environment, because they go further than merely improving the functioning of an area as a workers' dormitory.

A parallel view of social planning considers what the desired social structure of the city or neighbourhood will be after the plan has been carried out. For example, decisions can be taken on whether to keep a community intact or disperse it. Such decisions may have particularly far-reaching consequences when they concern communities of minority groups, and this goes a long way towards explaining the current sensitivity of the 'concentration or dispersal' debate in the race relations field. It now becomes an element of social policy whether certain kinds of communities are encouraged to disperse throughout the city limits, or remain as identifiable social and geographical groupings. This has been a continual preoccupation in the United States as well, where the Rand Corporation, amongst others, has attempted to develop programmes for the dispersal of minorities in the housing market.

The second recent tendency which points towards a coordinated attack upon the social planning problem is to be found in the crisis of confidence in the working of the Welfare State itself. While the middle classes perpetuate and feed off the myth that the workings of the social services in the last twenty years have largely brought about a redistribution of resources from rich to poor, and that those remaining at the bottom of society are there because of their own inadequacies and should be encouraged to stand on their own feet, they do more than perpetuate the old arguments which prevented social reform in the nineteenth century. Since the bureaucracy of the Welfare State was conceived, designed, and is manned almost entirely by the middle

29

classes, their own prejudice against its clients is likely to be a major determinant in its success or failure. It has been shown, for example, that more than half the cost of the National Health Service goes in salaries and pensions to those who operate it, while the recipients of weekly sickness benefit are actually worse off in real terms than before the war. It is relevant to ask therefore, as a number of people are beginning to, whether an increasing proportion of the cost of the Welfare State is going to those *doing* the welfare rather than those *needing* it. At the same time, through a deeply departmentalized bureaucracy, the manifestations of need are separately dealt with at the expense of a coordinated attack on the causes.

At the local level too, some hard questions appear to have been asked of the government services. At this level, however, rather more suggestions for reform have been forthcoming. The implications are clear. Public dissatisfaction with government and public services is most felt at their point of contact. Therefore piecemeal reform at the periphery of public contact – the local level – neutralizes the demand for more fundamental structural changes.

During the late 1960s government commissions produced reports on the state of education, the running of local authority social services, the management of local government, and on the reform of local government itself. Each of these reports in its way pointed to fundamental faults in the running of the bureaucratic machine, and proposed administrative reform through proper managerial coordination. Perhaps the most important document for the present argument is the Seebohm Report on local social services. This dealt explicitly with the problem of treating individual symptoms of need department by department, while a family's or community's problems remained untouched.

The Report recommended the setting up of new, co-ordinated social service departments which, with strong centralized management, will decentralize field-workers to offices in areas of major problems. This will enable improved communication and information channels with the public to be set up, and help to remove a hitherto intractable problem of lack of public knov. lege of welfare rights. Although still geared to the relief of need in the first instance, the form of the new department is clearly one which can go over onto the offensive in a war against poverty in a way that the previous methods of organization could never have achieved.

Organizational form has been a continual preoccupation of government as well as industry in the 1960s and, in particular, solutions to the problems of internal coordination and communication apparent in all large bureaucratic structures became a priority. As government has become more heavily committed to industrial and economic planning, it has found itself adopting more and more of the techniques of management originating in the business management schools, and the 'scientific' devices of corporate planning, planned programming and budgeting, systems analysis and other operations research techniques. Harold Wilson came to power in 1964 on a platform of 'Let's Get Britain Moving', and his administration carried through significant alterations to the civil service and departmental structure. Business management consultants were called in to advise on the running of state corporations and city organizations. The market-orientated techniques of industrial planning are merging with the more traditional forms of environmental planning. Thus a corporate management team for a city might now include the Clerk, Treasurer, Planning Officer, Director of Technical Services or Public Works, and the new Director of Social Services. Their main purpose: to prepare plans,

31

costing and programmes of implementation for every service offered by the authority, using the techniques and assumptions of the best business management practice.

Lessons are also being drawn for Britain's urban policy out of the North American experience which provides the background to Robert Goodman's own work. In the 1950s the Public Affairs Programme initiated by the Ford Foundation developed two approaches to the growing confusion in American cities. The first approach was through the reorganization of city government, and the second through urban renewal. Both of these sought to rebuild the social and economic ties between the city centre and the suburbs – the business and downtown areas and their surrounding slums and ghettos with the white middle-class suburbs. The programme sought to merge the increasingly divergent financial and administrative jurisdictions of the inner and outer city, (something Mayors Lindsay and Stokes were still attempting for New York and Detroit in 1970), while at the same time attracting back to the centre the more prosperous businesses and residents. The strategy was in many ways similar to the creation of a Greater London government and its own subsequent reversal of post-war decentralist policies. It is significant, however, that in the United States the initiative came from a charitable foundation in the first instance rather than from the Federal Government.

As in London, the main focus for the Ford Foundation's programmes were the so-called 'grey areas' analogous to our own 'twilight areas'. The programmes were followed by others which attacked the relationship between youth, delinquency and unemployment, underemployment and low educational attainment. All of these were considered important factors in increasing the social mobility of the poor and improving individual achievement. By the end of 1964 there were seventeen Community Action Agencies financed either through the Ford Foundation, or through the President's Committee on Juvenile Delinquency. These agencies in turn introduced a wide range of experimental reforms and innovations. They introduced vocational training and employment services, legal aid and community service centres. Both in their organization and in their programmes these early projects were models for the Community Action Agencies set up under the Economic Opportunities Act of 1964. It was under this Act that projects were intended to be undertaken with the 'maximum feasible participation'* of the residents. All these programmes recognized that the historical functions of the city had become decentralized to the point where the central city could no longer function either socially or economically. Thus, urban renewal would help to rebuild the city's central market places, and bring 'balanced' communities and wealth back to the inner core. The Poverty Programme would attempt to create new openings for social advancement for the poor, and participation would be an important incentive for the cooperation of the communities chosen to test the programmes.

Clearly these early programmes were improvisations in the face of a developing urban crisis. Governmental organization did not have power to institute reforms over the heads of its constituent states and cities in the face of traditional hostility to any form of more direct governmental interference in the rights of localities to produce their own solutions in their own way. Nevertheless, the community-action and urban-renewal programmes set up in the early sixties provided some interesting comparisons and lessons for the Welfare State in Britain. The first was in the relative freedom to

*See Ch. VI, p. 204.

33

experiment and put together programmes of particular relevance to local problems which the community development agencies had, in comparison to the rigid and prescribed organization in the Welfare State model. The second and perhaps crucial lesson was in the reawakening of interest in community development techniques which the American programmes produced in British academic and government circles.

Britain has much experience of community development in its colonial past. Simply put, the technique is to provide people who are considered in some way to be 'underdeveloped' with small projects such as a road to build or a well to dig, around which new structures of social relationships, and leadership in particular, can emerge. In the cities, the device may be a pre-school playground to run, or a newspaper or community centre to organize, but essentially the reasoning remains the same. In a developing country, community development programmes may need to be undertaken to offset problems of adaptation in fast changing circumstances, such as the disintegration of tribal or communal life, or of adaptation to urbanized or competitive economies. Modifications of the technique can be used according to this argument to combat social disintegration and urban poverty in developed economies upset by the processes of technological change.

In 1968, the British Government made its own first tentative applications of these lessons in the field of poverty and urban renewal. The intervention did not come from any of the existing statutory agencies, from the local authorities or the Environmental or Social Service Departments of government. The Urban Aid Programme was inspired and directed by the Home Office, whose traditional concern has been with the internal security and stability of the state. To date, the programme has been experimental and has relied upon small grants to specified areas for the provision of low-cost social facilities, and a number of small community development projects. As lessons are learned, the programme will expand. It fits the traditional forms of government and administration well, and is obviously inspired by the USA's Poverty Programme and by the attempt to create grass-roots leadership and self-help through community development.

Linked with the demand for social planning, finally, is the tendency in all heavily bureaucratized and centralized societies for the people to demand involvement in the processes of policy-formulation and decision-making, and for the fuller accountability of public servants. However, just as the institution of planning mechanisms does not necessarily democratize the economy, so the creation of superficial pluralist mechanisms to give voice to the opinions of particular pressure groups does little to alter the existing power structure. Indeed, if such pluralist mechanisms as Goodman describes have failed in the United States, whose political system is more receptive to the formation of pressure groups and lobbies, how much less successful are they likely to be in the British situation, with its professional mandarins maintaining government continuity and conservative progress. Thus proposals such as those contained in the Skeffington Report* on participation in the planning process, which recommends the setting up of a community forum as a reference group for communication between planners and the communities they plan, can at best be a very minor improvement. It will certainly have little to do with actual *participation* in the planning process. If the reference group is to represent internally the existing pecking order of power groupings, then again, even as a purely symbolic device, it is unlikely to represent a credible redistribution of power. The middle

* *People and Planning*, H.M.S.O., 1969.

35

classes are organized, industry and commerce are organized, the poor are not.

The best way of illustrating the convergence of these tendencies is to look at the recent development of planning in one city, Liverpool. The city has been heavily engaged in urban renewal and especially slum clearance programmes since the early 1950s and has consequently reflected most of the changing attitudes and techniques associated with city planning. More recently, it has also experimented with urban community-development programmes, and with the technical approaches and 'social indices' to be used in measuring social improvement. A number of forms of community forum and community involvement have also been tried, without any real ingredient of citizen power. The City Planning Officer, an architect, planner and sociologist, believes that community development is a significant part of the planner's responsibility. In talking about the fragmented nature of local government organization, he believes that planners may be the only public employees in a position to see the whole picture of what needs doing in the city. On the strength of this understanding, he may have to initiate community development programmes as well. He is a persuasive advocate of the techniques of corporate planning and the other business management techniques already referred to, and it is not insignificant that the city has employed McKinseys, the American-based business management consultants, to advise on the restructuring of the council's services around a corporate management group of senior officers. Liverpool was also one of the first areas chosen for a Home Office community development project. According to the Leader of the City Council, the object of all this was the creation of 'an efficient machine' capable of planning the social structure as well as the physical structure of the city!

Traditionally, the techniques of town planning in Britain have been summarized as 'survey and research, analysis and plan, programme of implementation'. In the early days of post-war urban renewal this programme was confined to renewal of the physical infrastructure of the city, then extended to include 'social' facilities. Now, according to one senior planner at the Department of the Environment, 'the society we are planning for can be analysed through its system of activities and relationships', and a similar programme of research, planning and implementation applied in social planning. By this he means the 'sociological study of man, his relationships and his communities, the preparation of an overall plan, and the subsequent programme of implementation'. From that, of course, it is not a big step to the 'scientific' implementation of socialization or segregation policies, or of Bantustans.

Other propagandists for social planning have put forward proposals for controlled experiments to test its effectiveness, and indeed the first projects set up by the Home Office laid a heavy emphasis on programme monitoring and evaluation. One expert has even suggested that it is possible to measure the effects of such experiments 'not only in social terms, but also in terms of cost-effectiveness'. His idea is that given the costly nature of bureaucracies, the strategy of self-help applied to planning might be no more expensive than 'traditional methods of regulating social systems'.

All these views of the nature and function of social planning are important in that they come from planners or social scientists. They are, however, likely to be restricted by the professional's own view of his particular role. A wider interpretation of the possible function of social planning can be obtained from *After the Planners* and from the American experience in general.

The American urban and poverty programmes were Federally controlled through both management and financing. As the *New York Times* reported in November 1965:

Maximum feasible participation by the poor in the anti-poverty programme is called for by the law. In the Budget Bureau's view, this means primarily using the poor to carry out the programme, not to design it. . .*

This, too, fits Goodman's thesis in that pluralist mechanisms were clearly not intended to bring about redistributions of power by those actually devising policy at the Federal level, however much idealistic reformers and community organizers tried to make participation a reality at the grass-roots level. Again, the Home Office programme follows this practice by keeping both financial and managerial control of the structure of its projects, leaving only details to be settled locally. It is therefore necessary to look at the possible motivations of the Federal government in setting up the local projects, to gain a clear idea of what it is all about. Daniel Moynihan conjures up his images of the 'next generation of poor urban blacks' being transformed into a 'stable working class population of truck drivers and mail carriers'.† Ex-Justice Earl Warren sees the ills of the ghetto as resulting from unemployment, and sees education as the imparting of 'the skill necessary for successful competition on the market'.§ The parallel with Victorian views of the 'shiftless poor' is striking. So is the comparison with Beveridge's fifth great evil – idleness. *Business Week* wants to see the slums and ghettos opened up for private enterprise as profitable markets.

* Quoted in *Dilemmas of Social Reform*, Peter Marris and Martin Rein, Routledge & Kegan Paul, 1967.
† Ch. VI, p. 206.
§ Ch. I, pp. 70–71.

If technological progress is going to create new markets, new demand-patterns and new techniques of production and distribution, it is also going to lead to new divisions of labour, and new patterns of social dependency. Yet this produces an inconsistency for the system. Continuous growth implies bigger markets for consumption, or increased rates of consumption for the goods and services produced. There are, however, not only residual pockets of low-consumption potential (poverty) from the past, but fresh pockets being created in the present. Just as it was necessary for capitalism to promote public health and town planning machinery to ensure a strong and reasonably contented labour force when manpower was a capital input to primary and secondary industries, so it was necessary for the system to devise new methods of economic and state planning to minimize the imperfections of the free market system for complex production and distribution. The effects of such reorganization can only last for a limited time however, since the essential irrationality of competition, production for faster consumption, and economic growth will soon take up the slack in the system thus gained. It then becomes necessary for planning to take place on the consumption side of the equation, and no longer through the 'soft' totalitarianism of advertising and the creation of markets for products. Pockets of poverty and underdevelopment represent imperfections for the market which must be removed, if the technostructure is to move away from war-orientated economic policies as the mainstay of future growth. Thus social and welfare planning will be a device increasingly used to ease out and finally eradicate imperfections of consumption. This will include the more efficient consumption of welfare and social security, as well as the more obvious forms in goods, commodities and services.

THE ROLE OF THE PLANNING PROFESSION

If it were suggested to planners, in Britain or America, that they functioned as part of a system of repression, their reaction would be likely to be one of outrage. Yet most would accept the propositions put forward by Moynihan and Warren for the use of planning and social policy to create new opportunities for self-advancement and social improvement *within the terms of the present society*. Many would also accept the parallel proposition that there are ethical as well as practical reasons why people should stand on their own feet and be self-supporting. This philosophy of 'personal salvation' effectively minimizes each individual's responsibility to a community, except in so far as those who are considered to be members of that community gain membership by their own unaided efforts. Thus it comes about that the apparatus of the Welfare State, for example, has benefited the middle classes and maintained the distribution of power and resources at its previous level.

Indeed, as a corollary of the fact that planning has not been an attempt to recast society in any fundamental respect, it has become one of the mainstays of policy for both the established left and right in British politics. Its development as part of the Welfare State apparatus has been supported by every post-war government. Planning is a part of the consensus and has therefore fallen into the conservatism of Daniel Bell's 'end of ideology' arguments.* As part of the consensus, the issue of whether or not to plan can be taken out of politics, and discussion of the nature of planning becomes depoliticized at the same time.

*Ch. VI, p. 201.

It is not surprising, therefore, that the planning profession has found it easy to be 'apolitical'. Since most are government servants, they have picked up the conservative traditions of the civil service as good functionaries to successive political groupings. Since these political groupings do not disagree on the essentials of the job the planners are doing, there has been minimal disturbance to their professional neutrality from that quarter. Most practitioners in the planning field in the inter-war and immediate post-war years were technical professionals, relying on such skills as surveying, building, civil and public-health engineering and law in contributing to the planning of cities, and therefore ill-equipped professionally to question the nature of their political role.

The only wider perspectives, in a professional sense, were brought by the architects who entered planning at the same time. Whatever the standard of their art they were subject to the prevailing belief-systems, building monuments to corporate or civic pride, or functional environments with high social purpose. Robert Goodman has devoted an important section of his book to the nature and effects of 'repressive architecture', and it is unnecessary to repeat the indictment here. Most architecture in our cities falls far short of the modern movements theories, and if one benefit of town planning in Britain has been to save our cities from some of the worst American excesses, it has been achieved through the maintenance of a drabness and conformity which may in the long run be worse. If the problems which Goodman cites have a familiar ring to them for the British reader, it is because the gods of architectural fashion are international, and the ideology they subscribe to is élitist and paternalist at best.

More recently, there has arisen a new profession, that of the 'pure planner', who traces his pedigree back

41

to Ebenezer Howard and the Garden Cities Movement, Raymond Unwin and Patrick Geddes. These men, leaders in the struggle to establish town planning at the turn of the century, have handed down a tradition of conceiving the design and layout of cities as whole entities, rather than being concerned with the development of particular components of the environment, such as roads or buildings. The methodology adopted by these early pioneers has led the profession subsequently into adopting scientific method and objective planning. Given the time-scales involved in creating and then implementing a town- or city-plan, it is not really surprising that a means had to be found for saving the professional and his work from the fortunes of public opinion and accelerating social change.

Patrick Geddes devised an empirical methodology which has been handed down to several generations of planners as 'survey, analysis, plan and implementation'. The formulation has become a crutch for the profession in times of trouble. If the surveys are done properly, then the facts of the situation will be incontrovertible, and an objective analysis will enable a feasible (i.e. non-controversial) plan to emerge. The problem, as Goodman has pointed out, is that facts cannot be separated from a particular set of ethics (legal or otherwise) and the constituency that uses them.* Used in this sense, of course, *facts* and *common sense* go together. Since the political consensus is based on the proposition that those areas of policy on which all political parties agree are just common sense and arise out of the nature of the situation, then this too has firmly wedded planning to the consensus view of politics.

The pure planners, particularly those educated in the post-war schools of planning, were quick to seize on the implications of the kinds of scientific method advocated

*Ch. VI, p. 199.

by Rexford Tugwell in the USA.* Since town planning developed professionally out of the working together of a number of related professions, as the scope of planning widened, so did the pressure from other disciplines, not all of them professional, to join the professional planning élite. Economists, geographers and social scientists in particular, whose work was bringing them with increasing frequency into the field of regional and economic planning, demanded recognition from the professional institute involved in planning. This was not willing to accommodate the newcomers. A professional group, personified by its institute, which was formed less than fifty years previously, was already failing to develop with the changing nature of its own professional practice. Yet it did not attempt to justify its position collectively in terms of theory or general propositions about the nature of planning, which would justify its exclusion of certain groups. Those individuals who did make the attempt were not agreed whether planning was a *field of activity* or a distinct *professional skill*.

In answer to this dilemma, one planner trained in the new schools argued that the profession should adopt the general approaches of operations research, and the specific device of systems analysis, as the basis for 'an intellectual approach to comprehensive planning, and clarifying its real nature'. Through this the professional identity of the planner would become more clearly defined. In fact, this solution was to prove prophetic for the direction planning would take in the 1960s, and fitted exactly the mood of other fields of government which were becoming concerned with efficiency and management techniques. Using operations research techniques, a more balanced view of planning would enable the urban 'system' to be understood, however simplistically. Programmes and priorities could then be

*Ch. VI, pp. 197–201.

devised for efficient city management, with planning in the forefront. The implications of this development have already been seen in the case of Liverpool.

The new planning professional, too, has effectively disqualified himself from any direct responsibility for his role in the wider political economy. In adopting a problem-solving stance professionally, he is free to maintain his neutrality and at the same time deal with those issues which the consensus identifies as 'problems'. These have to be easily identifiable, and open to 'feasible' solutions. If the planner strays far outside this brief, he invites conflict and calls his own neutrality into question. Thus his success or failure, even within the system's own terms, depends to a great extent on the way in which the problems and symptoms of the society manifest themselves. In order for him to act, it is not enough for a problem to exist: its existence must be recognized by those power groups for which he works. Therefore his assumptions and working-context are implicit in the maintenance of the present techno-structure. If he attempts to forestall the next crisis without proper sanction, that might involve an attack on the status quo which would not be allowed.

ROBERT GOODMAN'S VIEW OF LIBERATION

A number of questions were set out at the beginning of the Introduction which were relevant to an interpretation of Robert Goodman's thesis by those more familiar with the British experience of planning. Clearly there has not been space to set out the arguments in the detail that they merit, for on almost every page of *After the Planners* is some case history or insight which can be directly applied to a similar British example. Whatever the differences in administrative forms between British and American government, it is clear that, in common with other capitalist states, there has been a converging identity of interest between business and government. The growth of planning during the same period has been government's response to the expressed needs of business. Thus, planning is as deeply implicated in Britain as in the United States in the growing totalitarian tendencies of the technostructure. On the other hand, it is necessary to measure the intentions of planning against its actual performance. Although in theory the success or failure depends to a great extent on the power of the group or section of society being planned for, as against the power of the group advocating the planning (not always the same thing), in practice, planning has yet to develop the necessary techniques for a successful completion of its primary functions. It must be admitted that even within the terms of the present system, planning has not performed very efficiently in taking the jolts out of change. It is for this reason that the gradual take-up of business organization techniques by government is so significant. It increases the probability of a better match between public and private sectors, but on the terms of the private sector. Evidence of the relative success of the techniques applied to a particular field (where there was clearly a profit motivation) can be seen in the efficiency with which America has performed in the space race, or in the field of armaments (wasteful as these may be from other perspectives). In no case, however, has planning been involved in overt attempts at structural reorganization within the society.

Similarly, as the scope of planning increases to include widely divergent fields of activity, it is necessary to ask what we mean by 'the planners'. It is possible that the public at the receiving end of urban planning, for example, are correct when they identify as *planners* those who would previously have been given the general label *bureaucrat*. If this is the case, then it is unfair to single out as the major villains one particular group of professionals who, for mainly historical reasons, have become identified with environmental planning. On the other hand, as a group in society responsible for early attempts at coordinating the solutions to urban poverty and decay, it is surprising that few radical critiques of their role have been made, either within the profession itself, or before a wider audience. If planning does indeed have the critical importance for the maintenance of the capitalist system that Goodman's arguments indicate, then this is surprising, and perhaps also disturbing.

Throughout the book there are indications of the conflicting pressures to which planners in the American situation are subjected, and their own tendencies once under pressure. The interest shown by professional planners, and not only in the urban field, in the concepts behind advocacy-planning and community self-determination shows the extent to which many are aware of the dilemmas. In particular, young professionals and students left their offices and schools in droves to work alongside community groups and attempt to make 'maximum feasible participation' a reality. It was not their fault that their idealism was cynically used by the Establishment to add credibility to a criminal confidence trick. Most retreated, disillusioned, back to college or a 'straight' job. Even the university-sponsored projects were discontinued or re-orientated, and faculty members were sacked in the right-wing backlash against radical action emanating from the ghettos.

Robert Goodman's presentation of the evolution of a radical shows how, having started by trying to bridge the gap between the system and those outside it, he found, like most others who have attempted the same feat, that there is no middle way. The situation forces one to take

46

sides, even if in the end one gives up the struggle and acquiesces quietly. Once outside the system, it is easy to fall prey to apathy and helplessness in the face of the enormity of the situation and the task ahead. Alternatively, it is possible to lapse into meaningless acts of destruction and violence, as a means of defiance. This has, of course, been known all along by the poor and the oppressed, and is the first lesson to be learned by those who would join them in their struggle for liberation.

Yet this is understandable in the light of one further truth about the nature of the consensus in which planners operate. In the light of their own cultural backgrounds in the middle- or successful working-classes, their refusal to go along with the consensus appears merely wilful or neurotic, both to themselves, and to their friends, families and colleagues. This accounts for the schizophrenic activities of so many would-be radical planners in America and in Britain. For in Britain, too, planners and architects have been engaging for some time in the same kind of struggle that Goodman describes. The struggle has been less open for a number of reasons: the closed nature of the profession in Britain; the vocational nature of its training, which tends to make students study only those techniques currently in use; and the lack of any system for funding community projects other than through the existing government channels, which make even subsistence salaries impossible for would-be advocate planners. Thus it is that, while a growing number of community organizations are helped by inexperienced planning-students who are no match for the professionals they are up against, the graduates such students become unfailingly enter the government camp. That is not to say that all connections with community planning thereupon cease. On the contrary, there are many cases where young professionals are working for local authorities during the day-time, and for community associations, squatter groups, or the radical left during their spare time. The tensions in such a situation are obvious.

Given the position in which Robert Goodman and others find themselves, and in Goodman's case, the nature of the arguments which take him there, how important are his ideas for a *new professionalism* and *guerrilla architecture*. It is the kernel of his reasoning that, knowingly or otherwise, the compliance of planners in the systematic organization of society to suit the needs of the technostructure helps to extend the area within which, as Marcuse puts it, 'not only the socially needed occupations, skills and attitudes, but also individual needs and aspirations' of the whole population are predetermined. Bourgeois social theory, masquerading under such guises as *balanced social structure* or *opportunities for social mobility,* is the basis for such planning. The environments which it creates are themselves both a reflection and partial determinant of the efficiency with which the system reaches its goal, and the planner, as hybrid administrator and political operator, plays a crucial role in attempting to articulate these relationships.

In order to change this situation, it is necessary for those people most affected and least able to protect themselves to gain a new set of awarenesses about themselves and their predicament. A prerequisite of such a new consciousness will be the ability of people to exercise control over their own affairs, to act and choose for themselves, to mould rather than be moulded by the forces of change. If we claim the right for people and communities to be instrumental in bringing about social change, rather than having the change imposed from elsewhere, then we are establishing the right of each individual, in association with his fellows, to act and choose how his life shall be spent and his environment

48

controlled. The condition of deprivation is one which prevents the exercise of such choice, and therefore deprives some of an essential element of their humanity. This fundamental inequality of an impoverished urban life-style can no longer be tolerated if our view of ourselves as civilized and humane beings is to be sustained.

If the poor are to bring about the necessary changes in the institutions and structure which, implicitly or explicitly, block opportunities for advancement and self-determination, they can only do this collectively, not as individuals. Through organization, groups and communities can relate coherently to outside forces and pressures. If self-reliance is an important first step in the new consciousness, then it will be necessary to develop new institutions within the community or group, responding to its needs and under its direct control. Such groups must nevertheless be given help in organizing and in forging the tools necessary for their struggle.

A second pre-condition for a saner form of society is for intellectuals and professionals alike to desert their present roles, and put not merely their skills but their status directly at the disposal of such organizations and groups of the poor. In so doing, a new set of relationships must be established, which would increase rather than decrease the likelihood of the rules of the game being changed, so as to include the poor. The professional, leaving behind the privileges and symbols of his former position, joins with the people in a *joint educational process*. The injustices and inconsistencies of the society must be confronted where they occur in everyday life. If guerrilla architecture demonstrates more than just the powerlessness of people to create their own environments and life-styles, and also passes on new skills as a shared experience, then it is a small step on the road to liberation and necessary cultural change. The group of English planners who have adopted the maxim that 'No

49

just plan can be conceived or implemented without the consent and willing involvement of the people most affected,' have taken the same first faltering step.

After the Planners demonstrates clearly the need for a rejection of obsolete symbols and values, but there are, of course, problems in constructing an alternative road. There is a tendency for the Establishment to respond to radical programmes or groupings by encapsulating key sections or personnel, thereby leaving the programme or group with no constituency of its own. Again, it is always difficult to know when an apparently new programme is capable of being turned into something that will achieve change, or whether it will turn inwards on its creators and become another 'welfare state'. It would not, after all, be a new role for radicals if they became the gatekeepers or 'softcops' for the system. The important thing is to learn, test, and if necessary, help to dismantle and start again. In taking the decision not to go along with the offered myths of *freedom* and *affluence*, radicals are unlikely at first to make major changes in Establishment control, but can do something to lay the foundations of a new reality. Goodman's book may not take us far along the paths of necessary change, but he shows in which directions those paths will lie.

* * *

I echo and salute Robert Goodman's Dedication to 'all those brave people who won't put up with it' as it is; and would add in particular George Clark and other friends in Notting Hill who have stimulated many, like myself, to question their professional commitments. The arguments on these pages I share with them; the flaws are my own.

JOHN A. D. PALMER
London
September 1971

INTRODUCTION

FIVE YEARS AGO I dropped out of city-planning school. At that time I was halfway through writing a Ph.D. dissertation about how cities should be designed. I wasn't part of the turn-on, tune-in, drop-out culture, and I had no "radical" political analysis of my work; I just felt I had found something better to do. Working with a number of other architects, city planners, engineers and other urban specialists, I offered my services to neighborhood people who were usually poor and sometimes black. Since that time I have come to realize that it was not lack of expertise that was at the root of these communities' problems. To find out what solutions were needed meant looking at why the present solutions, of which we seem to have an abundant supply, continually fail. This book is a result of that search.

What I believe emerges is an insistent pattern of arrogant and repressive programs by many prominent, and not so prominent, planners, politicians and corporate leaders, usually in the cause of solving what has been called the "urban crisis." The solution to this dilemma, I contend, lies not in replacing these men with better-trained experts operating in the same cultural, political and economic context but rather in effecting a radically different role for the urban expert in a radically different context.

It would be a mistake to misread my analysis as describing a perverse plan by planners for making miserable lives for the poor and the disenfranchised. The disastrous results of their efforts may not be intended by the planners (though this fact doesn't excuse them from responsibility for their mistakes). Rather, the results flow from their adherence to the conventions of a repressive social structure which is biased against the people their plans are supposed to serve. Many of those committed to this structure probably don't see it in nearly as ideological terms as I have described. That people don't view themselves working within so explicit an ideology, however, doesn't contradict the fact that they do promote it through their actions. In fact, it is in that very ability of a social organization to promote a repressive ideology while masking its effects in the mannerisms and rhetoric of "freedom," "democracy" and "opportunity" that we find one of the unique forms of repression in both this country and the Soviet Union. The planners' own form of ostensible "value free," "scientific" methods have contributed to this repression. Through this posturing, the real bias behind their plans, whether the bias is intended or not, has been obscured from the people they have affected.

Many of the criticisms I direct at the planners I have also directed at myself as a practicing professional. In fact, it was my own search for a role as a person with planning skills, in a movement of people trying to change this society, that motivated this study. In trying to work as both a practicing architect and a city planner, I have personally felt the compromises and the platitudes of a profession refusing to admit it sold itself out a long time ago to those who rule our society. In the media, in professional articles and at professional conferences, we still speak the rhetoric of building humane places for all people. Behind it all we want to build, we want our programs to be acted upon, we want to be heard. We don't think of ourselves as agents of the oppressors, yet we are not really that far from being the Albert Speers of our time. "I sold my soul like Faust," said Speer, thinking about his past job as Adolf Hitler's personal architect, "to be able to build something great."[1]

As ostensible technicians, we are not the visible symbols

of oppression like the military and the police. We're more sophisticated, more educated, more socially conscious than the generals—we're the soft cops. Planners want "social change"; they deal in words, drawings, programs and buildings, not guns and napalm. But the kind of "social change" they usually find themselves dealing with, whether or not they recognize it, is organizing the oppressed into a system incapable of providing them with a humane existence, pacifying them with the meager welfare offerings that help maintain the status quo. At best we help ameliorate the condition produced by the status quo; at worst we engage in outright destruction.

Nor are the poor the only ones who have felt the weight of our programs. Young middle-class people, like the poor resident living in the center city, find themselves *reacting to* existing conditions rather than being able to initiate their own. For the middle-class student, the issue might be reacting to the institutionalized environment of his school; for the low-income in-town resident, it may take the form of

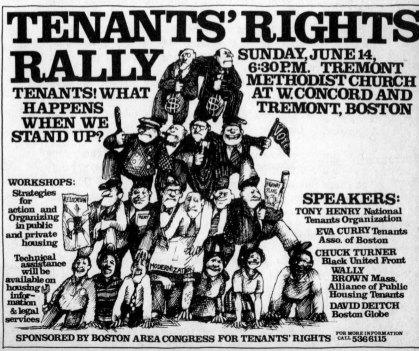

TENANTS' RIGHTS RALLY

TENANTS! WHAT HAPPENS WHEN WE STAND UP?

SUNDAY, JUNE 14, 6:30 P.M. TREMONT METHODIST CHURCH AT W. CONCORD AND TREMONT, BOSTON

WORKSHOPS: Strategies for action and Organizing in public and private housing

Technical assistance will be available on housing information & legal services

SPEAKERS:
TONY HENRY National Tenants Organization
EVA CURRY Tenants Asso. of Boston
CHUCK TURNER Black United Front
WALLY BROWN Mass. Alliance of Public Housing Tenants
DAVID DEITCH Boston Globe

SPONSORED BY BOSTON AREA CONGRESS FOR TENANTS' RIGHTS FOR MORE INFORMATION CALL 536 6115

reacting to the threat of urban renewal proposed by the city rather than being able to create his own housing programs. By this I don't mean to imply oppression of the poor is the same as that of middle-class students. The nature and intensity of the deprivation suffered by the poor is obviously not that of the materially more comfortable situation of the students. What impresses me, however, is the rigidly defined ritual of political participation in both cases and the resistance of those in power to making any basic changes in this ritual. In my experience school officials are usually "interested" in what the young people have to say—they "welcome" recommendations. Urban-renewal administrators frequently speak of "citizen participation" and "planning with people." Yet, the final decisions after the public hearings are made by those in power.

Former Chancellor Kurt Georg Kiesinger of West Germany described what is perhaps the classic "liberal" attitude toward the young of those in power:

> We must not meet these young people in an attitude of self-assurance and self-esteem. The young must *feel* they are listened to. *Our* task is to know that responsibility *is still in our hands,* and at the same time to be open to the arguments of the young people.[2] (author's italics)

Louis B. Lundborg, head of the world's largest bank, the Bank of America, and former Vice President Hubert H. Humphrey set the matter straight on this side of the ocean. According to Lundborg:

> We don't necessarily have to buy everything the young people are saying. . . . We do have an obligation, not only to them but also to ourselves, to listen to what they are saying and to examine it in terms of our own selves. But above all—communicate.[3]

And according to Humphrey:

> I think this younger generation has got something to say to us, and I'm not sure that what they say all the time is

necessarily the final word. I always believed in the right of a person to speak. I don't think he always has to be taken seriously, but he ought to have a right to say what he wants to say.[4]

That is, those in power can afford to let everybody talk as much as they like because in the end they decide who should be taken seriously. But it took President Richard M. Nixon to put the crowning touch on the idea of "communicating." On September 25, 1969, Nixon signed a declaration stating:

> Young and old, we are all Americans, and if we are to remain free we must talk to each other, listen to each other, young and old alike. . . . Now, THEREFORE, I, Richard Nixon, President of the United States of America, do hereby designate the period from September 28 to October 4, 1969, as National Adult-Young Communication Week.[5]

The next day Nixon held his famous press conference at which he discussed the October 15 Vietnam Peace Moratorium. "Under no circumstances," he told the press, would he be affected by the demonstrations.

This attitude of condescending "communication," of "keeping the channels open," has become the mainstay of the institutions which now rule our society. The growth of what is popularly called "the Movement" is to a large extent a reaction against the bureaucratic and centralized control of these institutions—a control which, as I will attempt to show, is maintained by so-called "progressive" city-planning techniques. These techniques have in fact been more conducive to maintaining profit-making environments and autocratic governments (in some socialist as well as capitalist countries) than to creating the more immediate and personally satisfying life conditions which many people are seeking. In my view, we can't wait for those who now rule to meet the demands for this change—they simply have too much to lose by doing so. What people *can* do is begin this process of change themselves. It is a process which should both examine the cause of our present condition and pose new ways for building more humane places to live. This book is directed toward that process.

I

With
a Little Help
from the Experts

The contemporary planners inherit a proud tradition of service, an egalitarian ethic, and a pragmatic orientation to betterment that are as old as the early social reform movements that spawned the profession. The caretaker of the idea of progress during the long years when it lay in disrepute in respectable quarters, the planner is now being wooed as the Cinderella of the urban ball. The resulting marriage of the social sciences and the planning profession holds out the promise that a new level of intelligence will be merged with noble purpose, in confronting the problems and the opportunities of the day.[1]
> —Melvin M. Webber, Former editor of the American Institute of Planners *Journal*

"Uh, oh, here comes the maps."
> —Neighborhood resident responding to the introduction of a city planner at a meeting in Boston

"TO HELL WITH URBAN RENEWAL," read an enormous sign on the front lawn, all but blocking out the small house behind it. The sign, which went on to warn "WE WILL DEFEND OUR HOMES WITH OUR LIVES," startled passing motorists with its official governmental style for announcing public projects. The house, one of a cluster of modest frame buildings, sat

opposite Harvard University's coliseum-like football stadium near the Charles River in Boston. A few years later across the same river in the city of Cambridge, famed for its academic strongholds of both Harvard and MIT, hundreds of homes, small stores and churches displayed the slogan "Cambridge Is a City, Not a Highway."

The urban-renewal sign in Boston represented a small beleaguered group of poor white families protesting the city's plan to tear down their homes in order to sell the land to a private developer for luxury housing. In Cambridge, the people were displaying their outrage at the state's plan to build an eight-lane highway through the middle of their neighborhood, uprooting thousands of poor people from their homes and jobs.

Five years ago, along with a few other city planners, architects and other urban experts, I began to work for both of these neighborhoods. We argued their cause before government officials at a multitude of public meetings. We criticized the professional competence of the official plans and presented alternative plans that we prepared after consulting with people in these neighborhoods. Our initial suc-

cess in helping neighborhoods stall government plans was publicized by newspapers and television. Soon other embattled groups began asking for our services. We formed an organization called Urban Planning Aid and, with the help of other volunteer urban experts and a small staff paid for by private foundations and government grants, we began to expand our work.

It seemed we had found an important way for professional planners to be relevant to some very important social problems. Expertise at the disposal of the poor was going to counter the arguments and programs of the government's bureaucrats. In the process, the injustice of these government programs would become apparent, and plans would have to change. We weren't alone in this belief. Since that time, the concept of providing professional help for the disenfranchised has spread not only in the planning profession but in fields like health, economics, and education. It's now even an accepted part of some government programs that the poor should have their own experts. Paul Davidoff, a city planner and lawyer and one of the first people to write about this kind of "advocacy planning" process, looked to it as a way of establishing "an effective urban democracy." By having the plans of many interest groups represented by planners, we would move, according to Davidoff, toward a pluralistic society.[2]

But, as I became more deeply involved in advocacy planning work, I began to have some serious doubts about how really significant it was all going to be. I began to question what a concept like "pluralism" meant in the context of our present American society. Though these questions arose in several projects and became more apparent to me in the research for this book, one project, which took us to Boston, stands out as an especially vivid microcosm of the dilemma.

We had gone to Boston's redevelopment office one summer morning back in 1966 to explain why our group was helping a neighborhood organization oppose the city's official plan.

That plan would have removed the neighborhood in order to build a new city-wide high school. Our small contingent of four planners made our presentation to Edward J. Logue, the agency's director, in his office overlooking the demolition and reconstruction of downtown Boston. We said neighborhoods should be able to choose their own planners and explained that such a process would make planning more democratic. He listened with a patient smile, asking only a few questions as he sat facing us from the end of his large conference table. When we finished, his smile vanished. "So long as I'm sitting in this chair," he said, "there's only one agency doing planning in this city, and that's this one!"

We tried again. When a high school is going to be located in a particular neighborhood, that neighborhood should at least be able to say where the school should go and what kind of housing should be built for those displaced. In this case the residents weren't even accorded the traditional subterfuge of "participation" in the plan. The renewal agency had simply prepared relocation plans to disperse them in a shotgun pattern to various parts of the city.

Logue's answer was that his planners were "as good as any that you have." But we were describing a *process* for planning, we explained, not personnel changes. It wasn't our "good guys" against his "bad guys." A local community should simply be able to hire or fire their own planners and not have to accept them just because they were provided by the city—whether or not it made the right choice of people was the community's problem. Logue said he appreciated the discussion and showed us to the door.

Later that summer, on a hot evening, the urban-renewal agency held a public meeting in the neighborhood designated for the high-school construction to "inform" the residents about its plan. City officials, knowing that the community had already been well informed, expected violence. Riot police were stationed outside the meeting hall.

What the officials found instead was an ordered and

articulate presentation of the neighborhood's demands. Presenting statistics and maps which we had helped prepare, residents of the area were able to demonstrate how the official plan hadn't addressed itself to their needs. While residents favored the high school, they said they also wanted a proper neighborhood to live in. They disputed the "technical studies" that were offered as supposed proof that the school would need large amounts of land and the claims that adequate measures would be taken in relocating families. They demanded that four hundred units of replacement housing be built in the same neighborhood. Visibly affected by the neighborhood's presentation, some members of the renewal board began discussions on housing.

Months later a new scheme was presented by Logue's planners. This time the setting was the City Council chambers. The city's plan now included a call for relocation housing in the neighborhood, but still it failed to specify when it would be built or how much the rents would be. During our testimony against this plan, one council member accused our group of being outside agitators, while Logue dismissed us as a "bunch of academic amateurs" who were trying to use the community as a "tinker toy."[3]

But the community wasn't to be put off by this attempt to divert the issue. They demanded a written agreement that relocation housing be built on vacant sites before people were asked to leave their present homes.

After more weeks of meetings with the renewal agency, a "Memorandum of Understanding" was finally signed by Logue, the Mayor and the neighborhood organization. As a result, the community felt it would have its say in who developed the area and how the relocation was to take place.

It wasn't until after seeing what happened to this neighborhood and others once the initial battle had been won, and the media fanfare died down, that I began to realize that advocacy planning and other forms of "citizen participation" could lead to another dead end. In the case of the high-school project in Boston, four years have passed as houses continue to run down, a good part of the community that originally fought the battle has moved from the area, meetings, meetings and more meetings have been held and still no housing has been built. A recent cutback in federal funds threatens still more years of delay. As one community organizer once said to me, "A brick hasn't been moved from one side of the street to the other."

In the case of the people with the "TO HELL WITH URBAN RENEWAL" sign, the last remaining holdouts were led from their homes by sheriff's deputies and tactical police in late 1969. After being told earlier that they would be able to stay, they were forced to leave for a "compromise" plan of middle-income housing that was to include a token number of apartments for low-income people. As for the Cambridge highway protest, the road is stalled, at least until the next election. Meanwhile, many of the original group of protesters have been forced out by rising rents caused by a severe housing shortage in the area. At the same time, another highway, which is to connect into the Cambridge one, continues to be built, making the inevitability of the Cambridge road all the more obvious.

These cases are hardly special situations. An advocate planner from New York called me not long ago and said he was making a film of advocacy projects around the country. Did I know of any projects he could photograph in the Boston area? My answer was no, since nothing had been built. I asked what kind of luck he was having in other cities. "I've called about everyone and everywhere I could think of," he said, "but there isn't anything. What does that say for advocacy planning?" "Not very much," I said. All he had done was confirm my own doubts about the possibility of relying on the availability of counter-professionals to bring about basic changes in our society.

As effective as advocacy planning might be in shifting some planning power to low-income neighborhoods and even occasionally stopping some governmental action such as a highway, these communities still have to operate within constraints set by those living outside their borders and whose interests are quite different from their own. To find answers to a community's impotence to effect changes in the way its people live requires looking at a more basic and more traditional dilemma than the lack of planning power. It currently goes under the nomenclature of "the urban crisis."

THE URBAN CRISIS: WATCHING AN OLD MOVIE

The Smithsonian Institution is weighing the possibility of adding a slum dwelling to its collection, which will be put on display, complete with dirt, dinginess, rodents, roaches, noise, odor, and broken artifacts.

—*Washington Post*[4]

I could include the usual litany of the population explosion, its effect on the city—tell you about the enormous amount of housing we must build in the next ten years to solve the sordid condition of our cities, their slums, their poverty and their crime. Then I could cap it all off with the once-over about the ugliness, the air pollution, the traffic congestion and the decrease of open space in our man-made urban world. But with *Life* magazine recognizing the urban crisis, after numerous Congressional investigations of urban problems,[5] and more than two thirds of us already living in urban areas, we might assume America is aware of the problem. It's hard for even academic types to keep up with all the university-sponsored symposia and conferences on the Crisis in the City, Cities in Crisis, the Urban Challenge, the Urban Crisis, Cities in Turmoil, etc., etc. At least one major university has gone so far as offering a government-sponsored program aimed at training people to solve city problems by equipping them for "urban survival."[6] At the American Institute of Architects' 1969 national convention in Chicago, there was even an "urban crisis tour," where architects were loaded onto buses and driven through the city's ghettos. One architectural magazine, in a straight-faced advance description of the arrangements, told architects that in addition to viewing the works of Frank Lloyd Wright and other noteworthy architects, they could "see a slum."[7]

If we are looking for ways to solve urban problems, what must concern us is not so much a continuing description of the crisis but an analysis of why we have the crisis in the first place. A traditional approach to defining these crises has been to see them as the inability of government and industry to harness technology in a way that would keep pace with the rapidly changing expectations and habits of the people. For example, inadequate methods for distributing resources lead to problems of poverty, and inadequate use of industrial techniques leads to ecological-environmental problems. Arthur M. Schlesinger, Jr., catalogued our national problems as no less than four crises: "the crisis of confidence," "the population crisis," "the ecological crisis" and the "urban crisis."[8] "Science and technology make, dissolve, rebuild and enlarge our environment every week," said Schlesinger, "and the world alters more in a decade than it used to alter in centuries." Following the argument of John K. Galbraith, he notes, "The acceleration of social change creates its problems without regard to systems of ownership or ideology. The great organization, for example, dominates Communism as much as it does democratic states. Indeed, more so," continues Schlesinger, "for the more centralized the ownership and the more absolutist the ideology, the greater the tyranny of organization." (Speaking of monolithic conceptions—Communist states are necessarily undemocratic, absolutist and centralized.)

Such a view of societal problems accepts our form of government and economic organization (our system of ownership and ideology) and sees societal problems as aberrations or "crises" resulting from the inability of technology and individual leadership to meet the challenge of something called the modern world. As Schlesinger puts it, "The crises we are living through are the crises of modernity. Every nation, as it begins to reach a comparable state of technical development, will have to undergo comparable crises." What we need, according to Schlesinger, is to "develop the intelligence, the will and the leadership to absorb, digest and control the consequences of accelerated technologies' change. . . ."[9] It is a familiar theme. Yet, in fact, the dilemma of our urban problems is hardly unique to modern times. It is in the basic traditions and values of American society that we find the root of this problem.

The cry of the urban crisis is really the echo of one which began with the Industrial Revolution. Civic leaders, decision makers, the power structures and the rest of the people that could be described by such phrases have been aware of city problems for many years. In 1856 a leading philanthropic organization raised a specter which sounds uncomfortably familiar today. Calling for improved housing conditions, it warned that the alternative was to have the poor "overrun the city as thieves and beggars—endanger public peace and the security of property and life—tax the community for their support, and entail upon it an inheritance of vice and pauperism."[10] It is out of such desperate fear of the effects of urbanization that the established powers have traditionally responded to the cry for reform.

DISEASES OF THE POOR

As planners today, we are the government's soldiers in a "war on poverty," directing our programs, in the welfare language, at "target populations." The turn of the century saw an important beginning to such programs. Publications with melodramatic titles like *The Menace of the Three-Decker* and *Room Overcrowding and the Lodger's Evil* were distributed by the National Housing Association, an early

America, 1889

housing reform group, while Jacob Riis's dramatic photo-journal *How the Other Half Lives* documented the sordid condition of human life in the city slum.

The "Housers," as these reformers were sometimes called, stressed the theme of overcrowding, open space, light and ventilation, fire protection and sanitation. Medical authorities had shown that periodic epidemics of typhoid, cholera, yellow fever and other more "day to day" diseases like tuberculosis were related to the congested and unclean conditions of the slums. Entranced with the reformers' medical research, the Housers would often concoct incredible speculations about how bad environment would affect social conditions of the poor. Poverty, some would argue, was not the result of an inadequate economic system, but bred on the conditions of the slums. Lawrence Veiller, one of the leading

67

Housers, rejecting the earlier view of social workers that poverty was a hereditary characteristic of the poor which could be ministered to but not cured, arrived at his own mythology. He described poverty as

> . . . a germ disease, contagious even at times; that . . . thrives amid the same conditions as those under which tuberculosis flourishes—in darkness, filth and sordid surroundings; and that when the light has been let in the first step towards its cure has been taken.[11]

The effects of years of public housing, with all its emphasis on fresh air, sunlight, parks and antiseptic buildings (where the barren tiled hallways have all the warmth and charm of an industrial toilet), are as dramatic a refutation of germ theories relating poverty to environment as one can imagine. The inhabitants of our dormitories for the poor have all the "symptoms" of poverty as those living in adjacent tenement areas, without even the consolation of the corner stores, storefront churches, street life and lack of bureaucratic administration of their old "slum." Yet the "disease" and slum-generating theories of poverty keep on coming. Almost sixty years after the Housers, Hubert H. Humphrey, when Vice President of the United States, was still using such theories to obscure the causes of poverty in this country.

Talking to a conference of mayors in 1966, Humphrey spoke of a new kind of "ism" we must fight against—"slumism." It is the "enemy within our gates," he said, just as the enemy without is communism. According to Humphrey's definition of slumism:

> . . . it is poverty; it is illiteracy; it is disease; it is discrimination; it is frustration and it is bitterness. . . . It is a virus that spreads, that races like a malignancy through our cities, breeding disorder, disillusionment, and hate. We simply must declare war on this evil, just as we have on Communist aggression.[12]

America today

Almost sixty years earlier, the First National Conference of City Planning was given an analysis similar to Humphrey's. Raising the specter of social upheaval and "socialism," Henry Morgenthau gave the following rationalization for city planning:

There is an evil which is gnawing at the vitals of the country, to remedy which we have come together—an evil that breeds physical disease, moral depravity, discontent, and socialism—and all these must be cured and eradicated or else our great body politic will be weakened. This community can only hold its preeminence if the masses that compose it are given a chance to be healthy, moral, and self-respecting. If they are forced to live like swine they will lose their vigor. We can imagine how much greater the exodus from congested areas would be if the newer districts were planned artistically and provided with proper parks, playgrounds, public baths, and decent mode of transit.[13]

In Humphrey's updated urban-crisis speech, he showed the streak of fair play that made him so popular with the liberals. "I happen to believe," he said, "that if there had never been a Karl Marx or Lenin or Stalin that there would still be many problems in this world that would terrify us and shake us out of our complacency." What he was saying is that "slumism" and other problems would be with us even if we didn't have communism!

As the myths about the causes of poverty were exposed, new ones have been created to take their place. Today, reformers and planners still talk about the need for more low-income housing. But with the failure to get rid of the poverty of those living in public housing, they temper their "bricks and mortar" approach with a call for more "people" or "social" programs:—a current favorite being the provision of jobs for the poor. On the conservative side, there is Richard Nixon's welfare program which would provide a maximum family allowance of $1,600 a year for a family of four. "The new family assistance," said Nixon, "would provide aid for needy families; it would establish a work requirement, and a work incentive; but these in turn require effective programs of job placement—including a chance to qualify not just for jobs, but for good jobs, that provide both additional self-respect and full self-support."[14]

Nixon's views on taking care of the poor complement those of one of the most liberal men to sit on the United States Supreme Court. "They are ignorant, they have had no schooling," said Earl Warren, former Chief Justice and former California Governor, describing the unemployed in the big city ghettos, "they have no skills with which to compete in the economic market, they are easy prey to all kinds of bad influences in the community." "We must get rid of the ghettos," he said, "we must see that every youngster who comes into being in our country is afforded a decent education and is given some skill through which he can compete in the market."[15]

"Compete" and "incentive" are the key words of both these visions. Workers are to be given enough incentives (a maximum of four hundred dollars a year for an adult and three hundred dollars a year for each child in the case of Nixon's welfare program) that they will continue to compete with one another for jobs which industry finds useful. Nixon's program would require welfare recipients to travel anywhere in the country that a job is available, so long as the employer paid travel expenses.

Hubert Humphrey wasn't just mixing his metaphors about disease and war, nor were he or Morgenthau or Nixon or Warren alone in seeing poverty, slums, bad education and the rest as "diseases," aberrations, the result of "bad influences" or anything but an integral feature of the American economy. Both liberal and conservative reformers, confronted with the products of this economy, as we will see, have usually come to similar conclusions. The economic system is right—something must be wrong with the people who don't fit it. Change the people who don't fit, cure *them* of *their* diseases, they argue, and the system will operate effectively. Today's "cures" are not simply jobs, but "jobs with a future," not simply capitalism, but "socially responsible capitalism." Today many leaders in government and industry promise that once we end our foreign "mistakes" like those in Southeast Asia, we can begin to provide such cures. What is needed supposedly is more perseverance, more research about what ails the poor, and especially more money. I suggest that before we accept this program for "working within the system," we should look at the performance and the vision of those who would entice us.

71

II

The Urban-Industrial Complex: PART ONE

It was obdurate government callousness to misery that first
stoked the flames of rage and frustration. With unemployment a scourge in Negro ghettoes, the government still
tinkers with trivial half-hearted measures, refuses still to
become an employer of last resort. It asks the business community to solve the problems as though its past failures
qualified it for future success.

> —Dr. Martin Luther King's last letter asking sup-
> port for his march on Washington[1]

Business and businessmen can do what no other segment
of America can do to benefit our people and improve the
country, if they become involved in the great social problems
of our time. . . .
  The time has come when we who believe in competitive
industry and enterprise must go among the people to make
clear that this system has given us everything we have and
it can give us everything we want.

> —Maurice H. Stans, United States Secretary of
> Commerce, 1969[2]

"THESE ARE NOT men who are anxious to kill people," said
George Wald, Nobel Prize biologist and popular anti-war
liberal, admonishing us to help the defense contractors in
their dilemma. "They're men who are anxious to make

Lightweight aluminum caskets from Vietnam

money. We've got to find other ways to make money. There are very serious practical problems. And the men in the defense industry have faced them. *We* haven't. *They* have."[3]

Wald's sense of urgency reflects a growing feeling, especially among liberals, that to get out of the business of such imperialist adventures as Vietnam we will have to turn industry's money toward peaceful domestic programs. Indeed during the past few years the major industries themselves, along with their supporters in government and the universities, appear to be hedging against peace, retooling themselves for a shift in emphasis; aerospace companies are examining prefabricated building systems, computer companies are producing teaching machines, electronics firms are designing transit systems, while aerospace and systems-analysis firms are devising more effective ways to control riots and organize systems of justice. Universities under the pressure of growing student protest are attempting to convert parts of their war research laboratories to urban research and other peaceful purposes. Some aspect of urban

73

studies is now part of most university course offerings, even if this simply involves a change in course titles. It is as though if it's not urban, it's not relevant and socially conscious—with the corollary that being involved in urban problems is somehow good *per se*. What may seem like a major trend of change toward peace and humanity by the institutions now associated with war and imperialism may appear as a consoling and optimistic picture of the flexible way our political system responds to protest.

If in fact a responsive "urban-industrial complex" could be formed to solve the problems of poverty, race, quality of life and other urban-crisis phenomena, this should give radicals pause in their determination to dismantle the present structure of American society. In this situation what the Left should do as humane, civilized people is not try to destroy capitalism but to help businessmen convert their resources. What is good for the country should be made good for General Motors.

Indeed, as George Wald said, business has faced the problems of conversion and will continue to do so. An urban-industrial complex is not so much a distant possibility as it is an accomplished fact—albeit on a more modest level than our military one. In such programs as housing, urban renewal, highway building, education and job training, there already exists an amalgamation of university, government and industry with experts in planning and architecture which has for some time developed programs to solve the urban crisis.

"Chicago has made more improvements than any other city in the United States"—Mayor Richard Daley

THE CITIES AS COLONIES

Some of Chrysler's applicants signed on for job training, then never showed up. Others who did report were notoriously late. As Chrysler registered those who did report, it found that many of them had never been counted in a census, had no social security number, had never registered to vote, and belonged to no organization of any kind. "In most of the accepted senses," Boyd (Chrysler's president) says, "they really didn't even exist."[4]

One doesn't have to look much beyond the propaganda of the corporations themselves to see the rationale for industry's involvement in the urban crisis. In a magazine written for American Airlines travelers (appropriately called *The American Way*) you will find industry's involvement in the ghetto put at least as bluntly as any New Left magazine might have done. In an article titled "Business Tackles the Ghetto," written to show how "big business is taking a major and growing role in the struggle of black men for economic equality," the author says:

> Some of the impetus for the growing involvement of big business in the ghetto is self-interest, of course. Executives are quick to admit that if the nation's big cities continue to deteriorate, corporate investments will be destroyed with them. Alternatively, companies view America's poor as a vast potential market.[5]

Meanwhile, a survey of 201 major corporations with urban-affairs programs demonstrated that the principal motive of nearly all companies was "enlightened self-interest."[6] According to this survey, in the *Harvard Business Review*, urban-affairs involvement was seen as a way of "strengthening corporate reputation and image."[7] Four fifths of the companies cited "appearance" as the reason for their involvement. Thus urban involvement becomes a major tactic in the corporation's strategy of business as usual. As one corporation head told a group of his fellow businessmen:

> We must not think of public interest motivation as sheer
> altruism, but rather as enlightened self-interest. Looking
> at the question negatively, what chance is there for free
> enterprise and democracy if the riots don't stop, if we
> cannot achieve a social order consistent with *our* ideals.[8]
> (author's italics)

And *Business Week*, a magazine hardly noted for Marxist
analysis of society, summed it all up in its predictions for
the Seventies. "A new breed of men will call the shots," says
the magazine. According to their crystal ball:

> . . . the top manager of the seventies will be increasingly
> involved in seeking solutions to the social problems of the
> environment in which his business must exist. But his in-
> volvement in social questions will stem as much from some
> sort of "enlightened self-interest" *in the continued wel-*

University of California, Berkeley

Vietnam

fare of his organization, social class, or family.[9] (author's italics)

With the disastrous political effects of the Vietnam war, the ability of the corporations to make profit on counter-insurgency and the cold war have diminished, yet hardly evaporated. What the corporations are looking toward is the "peace dividend," which could include a substantial source of government funds for urban problem solving. This will let many corporations continue their military profit-making while "diversifying" their markets in domestic areas. But on the urban front, the corporations will take on government planning programs only where they can garner from them the right combination of public relations, protection against revolution and especially profit. Thus if industry can find a way to profit, for example, from education programs for the poor (especially with government subsidies), then—leaving aside for a moment the educational content of these pro-grams—the poor could get some form of education from

industry's affairs. If it turns out that it's easier for the corporations to make profit by building highways, then that's the social product the poor and the rest of the population are likely to get—as well we have.

For the present and future some of our major urban products can be expected from the "law and order" corporations. According to *Moody's Stock Survey*, riots will nurture big business. The future for firms supplying protective equipment and services to police forces and industry, they say, "can only be considered bright."[10] They continue:

Spending for law enforcement approximated $930 million in 1967, $1.1 billion in 1968. *Time* Magazine expects such expenditures to grow at a 10% annual rate for the next several years. Newly aroused Federal interest, as ex-

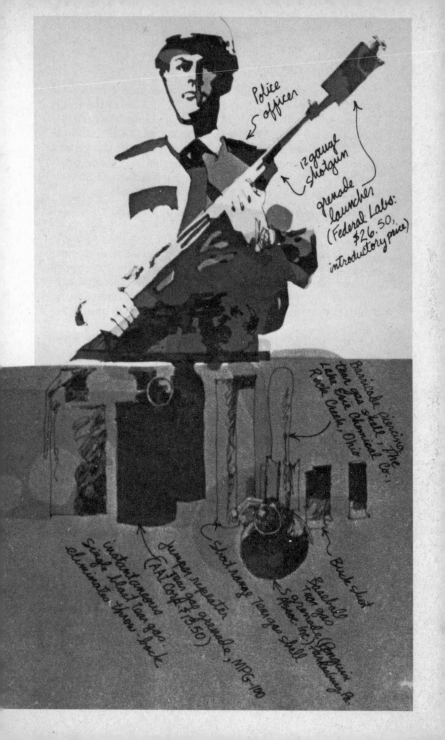

emplified in the June 1968 Safe Streets Act, is expected to
result in the infusion of several million dollars at the local
law enforcement level. The Act itself will increase Federal
anti-crime aid from the $63 million of 1968 to $500 million
in 1972. Bangor Punta, a leading company in the crime
control field, foresees a $5 billion market for police pro-
tection by 1975. The market is currently growing at a 9%
annual pace, even without Federal expenditure.[11]

Here is a partial description of Bangor Punta, a stock
recommended for purchase:

Among the company's major law enforcement tools are
safety helmets, Smith & Wesson handguns (the preferred
weapon for most police forces), riot control equipment
(Pepper Fog and Chemical Mace), resuscitators and a
standard testing device for determining driver intoxica-
tion.
    With total expenditures for public security rising
rapidly, Bangor Punta's leadership in this market makes
its common well worth holding for *long-term appreciation*.[12] (author's italics)

Yet even where the corporations and government shift
from cold war and counter-insurgency problems to such
relevant ones as "poverty," "education," "the environment,"
or "transportation," their solutions give little hope that
those who suffer most will benefit from these efforts. Rather
the direction of programs, paralleling the development of
the military-industrial complex, indicates the creation of
enormous bureaucracies with technocrats distributing government contracts to private firms as they themselves move
back and forth between their government jobs and these
same firms. We find powerful industrial lobbies which have
promoted and received incredible government subsidies for
their urban products—products which are often in direct
contrast to the needs of people. And we also find industry
controlling the very same governmental agencies which are
supposedly regulating them in the public interest.

80

To regulate environmental pollution, for example, forty states have created anti-pollution boards. But of these forty, thirty-five have officials who are at the same time officials in private corporations that are among the biggest industrial polluters in the country. Ranging in position from government board members to chairmen, these officials represent over one hundred firms, including Monsanto Chemical, Union Carbide, Du Pont, Stauffer Chemical, Scott Paper, United States Steel, Anaconda, Reynolds Metals, Aluminum Corporation of America, and the Weyerhauser Lumber Company. Rarely do these government boards contain more than one or two, if any, members representing the general public. To cite just a few outstanding cases, four of five members of Ohio's Air Pollution Control Board have ties to industries that pollute. All six "industry" seats in Alabama are occupied by executives from companies involved in pollution legal proceedings. The only so-called "public" member of Pennsylvania's eleven-member Air Pollution Control Board is the former vice president of a steel company. In Colorado, a state hearing on stream pollution by a brewery was presided over by the pollution control director of the same brewery.[13]

Meanwhile, on the poverty front, government programs, ostensibly aimed at helping the poor, provide a convenient financial conduit for poverty entrepreneurs who shift between private and public roles. By June 1970, one out of every four Office of Economic Opportunity (OEO) consulting, evaluation, technical assistance and support contracts were received by sixteen firms which among them employed thirty-five former anti-poverty agency officials. Citing just a few examples of the relationship between government officials and the poverty firms, we find Leo Kramer, a former associate director of the office of selection and training of one of OEO's programs, now head of Leo Kramer, Incorporated. Since leaving OEO, his firm has collected over two million dollars in anti-poverty contracts, several involving his former government department. Gary Price, who served with Kramer at OEO, became president of Policy Management Systems, Incorporated. The firm has received over 3.3 million dollars in anti-poverty work, including several contracts from his former department. Stanley Ruttenberg, in his role as manpower administrator in the Labor Department, gave Phoenix, Arizona, 3.5 million dollars in job training money. Two years after the grant, a firm he began after leaving the agency, Stanley Ruttenberg and Associates, was evaluating the same project for the city of Phoenix. Robert Levine, while director of OEO's research office, gave the RAND Corporation, the noted private consulting firm for the Air Force, two "sole source" contracts totaling 600,000 dollars. A sole source contract means that only one company can bid on the work. Before coming to OEO, Levine was a top executive at RAND.[14]

While government technocrats build careers and profits from the poverty business, the industrial corporations, spurred by their own "enlightened self-interest," have also moved into this enterprise. Touting the "profit motive" as a more efficient method than "bureaucracy" for shifting poor people into the mainstream of middle-class life, industry is now developing a strong foothold in poverty programs, job training, and education.

SCHOOL DAYS

ANN ARBOR, Mich.—John F. Soghigian, 25 years old, arrives at the University of Michigan for a five-day environmental teach-in. He is unshaven, his hair is mussed, and he's dressed in loafers, Levi's and an old sweater.

On campus he attends a rally sponsored by a radical group, drops in at a coffee house and seeks out radical-looking students for "rap sessions." "The longer their hair, the more anxious I am to get in contact with them," he says.

Mr. Soghigian is a public relations man for Dow

Chemical Co., ill-suited as he may look for the part. It's his job to attempt to gauge the mood on campus, present Dow's point of view to students and "learn what to expect and be ready for contingencies" when high-level officials of Dow venture on campus themselves for speaking appearances. . . .

To prepare for the latest round of teach-ins, Dow recently called another meeting of public relations men and officials who had been designated to represent the company as speakers. Executives' experiences at the University of Michigan teach-in were discussed, and then the officials threw practice questions at one another. Each man was given a packet containing official Dow responses to several controversial issues, including the company's involvement in napalm and herbicides.

The executives were cautioned, however, not to answer questions too quickly lest it become obvious they were reciting prepared answers. They were urged to think about each question "for five seconds" before replying.

The most troubling question was how to deal with the recent disclosure that a Dow plant at Sarnia, Ontario, had been spilling poisonous mercury into the St. Clair River and contaminating fish. As a result, U.S. and Canadian authorities have banned fishing in the St. Clair River and Lake St. Clair and in parts of the Detroit River and Lake Erie.

Dow officials at the briefing were unsure how to deal with the matter at teach-ins. "It shoots us down," said E. S. (Bud) Shannon, as waste control manager. "I haven't come up with an answer to that yet."[15]

—*The Wall Street Journal*

Kingman Brewster, Jr., the president of Yale University, recently wrote an introduction to a collection of campus lectures by Henry Ford II. Brewster spared no effort extolling the virtues of Ford's prescriptions. "Politicians, commencement speakers, hucksters everywhere," he said, "would do well to take a leaf, any leaf, from this book."[16] The image this evokes of the liberal college official support-

83

ing the views of a liberal businessman seems a fitting
scenario for our times. Indeed, many such college officials
have anticipated Brewster's advice; Ford's words must have
a familiar ring to those who, over the past few years, have
either sat at college commencement exercises or listened to
college officials during a "confrontation." Said Ford:

> Your generation seems intensely disillusioned not only
> with big business but also with big universities, big
> government and big organizations in general . . . I can
> assure you—and I know that President Brewster would
> agree with me—that big organizations are at least as
> frustrating to the people who administer them as they
> are to the people who are affected by them. On the other
> hand, we have to accept the fact that big organizations are
> here to stay. We cannot turn back to a simpler age and
> a smaller scale. We cannot decide whether or not to rely
> on big organizations; our only choice is whether they shall
> be better or worse. If the big ideals are not achieved
> through our major institutions, they will not be achieved
> at all.[17]

This now familiar exhortation for college youth to temper
their ideals to the existing structure of society, to "work
within the system," fits a well-worn model of the university
as the incubator for the corporations' future personnel.
Brewster, who describes Ford's ideas as exhibiting "practical boldness," makes the connection between the university
and business even more explicit. "The academy and business," he told a recent gathering of corporate executives,
"have a joint trusteeship for the freedom of the marketplace,
the ballot box and ideas."[18] Edgar J. Kaiser, chairman of
the Kaiser Industrial Corporation, one of the largest sup-
pliers of government war products, gave that same group
probably the best synthesis of the university-corporate
model. "Business needs education to reach youth," he told
them. "The challenge to business and education is *how to
motivate youth to believe the system holds the greatest*

opportunities for them."[19] (author's italics) Somehow, that admittedly honest view of education as a socializing process for "the system" hardly matches the often stated liberal view of the university as a refuge of free inquiry in danger of being perverted by campus radicals.

While universities train the wealthier, more "mobile" people for high-echelon business positions (the executives, management personnel, government bureaucrats and the professionals), they have relied on the elementary and high schools for lower-level personnel. But as the drop-out phenomenon continues, with school facilities becoming more difficult to maintain because of a low community tax base, the corporation increasingly finds itself either running its own training programs or actually "adopting" local public schools. As *The American Way* article cited earlier boasts:

In Detroit, Michigan, Bell Telephone Company and Chrysler Corporation each have adopted ghetto high schools. Northern High School, with 1,800 students, 98% of whom are Negroes, calls on Michigan Bell for man-power, technical and management skills and training facilities.

Chrysler's parental interest in Northwestern High School includes much of the same kind of help. In addition, Chrysler last year installed a modern, $150,000 garage at Northwestern to train auto repairmen.

Aetna Life Insurance Company has adopted a high school in Hartford, Connecticut, as have Bell System companies in Chicago and Milwaukee. Ford, G.E., Avco, and Procter & Gamble Companies recently adopted the entire 2,000 pupil school system in Lincoln Heights, Ohio, a mostly Negro suburb of Cincinnati.[20]

Another similar education program finds schools contracting directly with corporations to teach their children on a profit basis. This approach, called "performance contracting," is usually aimed at "problem students" and stipulates the company receive a fee per student on the condition it teach the student a certain amount of material. In Texarkana, Arkansas, for example, Dorsett Education Systems, beating out such competitors as RCA, McGraw-Hill, Westinghouse, IBM, and Singer, won a $250,000 performance contract to teach children in the local schools. The Thiokol Chemical Corporation of Utah, which uses Massachusetts Education Commissioner Neil V. Sullivan as its sole educational consultant, has $208,000 worth of performance contracts in Dallas, Texas, in addition to similar contracts in other cities. Sullivan, incidentally, interviewed as a public official at a press conference in Dallas, praised Thiokol's work in that city's schools. It was only after a reporter later asked Sullivan if he was Thiokol's consultant that the Dallas superintendent of schools said he learned of Sullivan's role.[21]

More disturbing than public officials lending stature to private corporation educational enterprises is the nature of this educational process itself. In the case of Dorsett's work in Texarkana, for example, the company is to receive $80 for each student who improves at an approved performance rate and a bonus of up to $27 for those who improve faster. When the student doesn't improve fast enough, the company will get less than its costs. Performance rates are to be judged by national tests that measure "grade-level" achievements.

By focusing education on those items which can be measured or tested, this incentive system for the corporations perverts what should seem an important concept of education. Improvement is geared not to a child's personal development needs but to certain levels of achievement tests which become the measure of whether a corporation should be paid or not. The student's ability to perform well on tests rather than his critical ability to judge and use information becomes the measure of achievement. Furthermore, to make a profit, the company must be efficient in its use of personnel; rather than spend time on the most difficult students, the "bounty" per head is an obvious inducement for the corporation to process those students who adapt most easily to their techniques.

But before children even enter public school, they can now expect business and its experts to be deeply involved in their education. Recent studies showing that preschool years are an important time in a child's receptivity to learning have

aroused parental, government, and business interest in preschool education programs. Franchise sellers and purchasers
of preschool child care centers throughout the country are
already collecting government money, and more of the same,
especially for poor people, can be expected if Nixon's welfare proposal is passed, putting into jobs approximately
150,000 welfare mothers who have about 450,000 children.[22]
Describing one such preschool program, developed by the
Universal Education Center (UEC), Ann Cook and Herbert
Mack, two former public school teachers, give a frightening
critique of what is happening.

The program developed by the Universal Education
Center locates "Discovery Centers" in middle-class communities where parents are worried about giving their
children a head start in school training. "Skills, not children,
are emphasized," say Cook and Mack. "How the child performs, not who he is, or how he thinks, becomes the focus."[23]
According to UEC's own brief for investors, their "Discovery Center" provides "educational consultants" and
"educational materials specialists." The "educational consultant" is a kind of education doctor who, according to
their brief, "periodically evaluates the educational development of the child much as the family physician gives check-
ups," while the "educational materials specialist" is called a
"salesman." Both develop a strong relationship with the
parents in order to sell UEC products. Again according to
UEC's own investors' brief, the educational consultant,

> . . . relieves parents of the bewilderment, worry and
> frustration which they feel concerning their children's
> educational development, and provides them with the
> guidance they need. He reassures them that they are
> doing right by their children and that by following his
> counsel, they are preparing their children for the world
> of tomorrow. . . .

After the prescription has been completed either in
response to an inquiry by the parent or spontaneously, the

Educational Consultant offers to put the parent in touch
with the UEC materials specialist. If the salesman is on
the premises at the time, he calls him in and introduces
him, for the purpose of scheduling a visit to the home.
. . . Or he offers to give the materials specialist the
parents' phone number. In any event the parent is later
contacted by a salesman.[24]

As UEC sees it, the kind of "trust" developed between the
educational consultant and the family can lead to all manner
of profitable ways to exploit parents. According to their
brief again,

> . . . it goes without saying that the consultant who has
> the family's trust in matters of education and child rear-
> ing will also have their trust in matters not pertaining to
> education directly.
>
> If UEC offered other products and services, such as
> travel agency services, home furnishings, hobby products,
> household products, special food products, life and other
> insurance, etc., it would be in an excellent position to sell
> these to its clients. The opportunities for horizontal in-
> tegration at the product level are fairly staggering.[25]

Fairly staggering, indeed. But this educational Trojan horse
for consumerism is not without its professional "experts" to
lend it respectability. UEC's national advisory board includes Wilbur Cohen, a former secretary of the Federal
Department of Health, Education, and Welfare, Martin
Deutsch, director of New York University's Institute for
Developmental Studies, and Robert Glaser, director of the
Learning Research and Development Center at the University of Pittsburgh.

In cases where corporations set up their own ghetto educational job training programs, it is often done with the help
of government funds. When Avco built a plant in Roxbury, a
black section of Boston, it received over a million dollars
from a federal grant to train 200 to 250 "hardcore unemployed." According to *Fortune* magazine, Control Data,

Goodyear, General Dynamics and Northrop are contemplating similar approaches. So profitable are some of the training programs that firms created for this purpose now bid with each other for government contracts. One firm, called MIND, Inc., a subsidiary of the Corn Products Company, expects to have a $10 million business in five years. It already has contracts with IBM, Procter & Gamble, Crown Zellerbach and Chrysler to train unemployables.[26]

In North Carolina, the Radio Corporation of America (RCA), under a subcontract with a local poverty agency, is attempting to give seasonal workers and migrant farm workers "salable skills." "RCA and fifteen or twenty other large corporations," says Dr. Charles Moffett, project director, "have realized the government needs help in developing our human resources. These corporations also have products to sell, so it's a realistic business venture to create a market. Anyway," continues Dr. Moffett, "with a three-billion-dollar income and 130,000 employees RCA is the government."[27]

This "government's" brochure says their training and rehabilitation program is to be carried out in "an atmosphere that fosters the development of self-concept and evaluation within the individual." But the real purpose of the training comes in what RCA calls "modification of behavior." As a result of their training, according to Fletcher Lassiter, counseling coordinator, "they start pluggin' with a whole different mode of living. Independence, I guess."

What this "independence" and "self-concept" meant was modifying their behavior to fit jobs which happened to be needed locally. But the market for these jobs dried up after only twenty-five families completed the course. To solve this dilemma, RCA is trying to coax other companies to move into the area with promises of training their labor force.[28]

Operating their own training programs for the "hard core" requires that RCA deal with "special problems" not

90

often found with the more "motivated" workers, those who have had a "successful" education. Not only does the corporation decide the kinds of skills these workers will be taught, but it must look after their personal lives as well. Describing RCA's training program, *The American Way* article notes:

> In dealing with the hard core, "it's necessary not only to reach out to get them, but also to dip into their personal lives" to keep them on the job, says Frank McClure, personnel vice president at Radio Corporation of America. Mr. McClure says RCA personnel men often go to the homes of newly hired hard-core employees who don't show up for work.
>
> An RCA plant personnel man on such a visit found that an eager, hard-working youth's record of absenteeism was caused by an older unemployed brother who kept stealing the young man's clothes. The problem was solved shortly afterwards when police jailed the older brother on other charges.[29]

Rationalizing this dipping into people's personal lives in more professionally acceptable language is the job of the government's poverty planning technocrats. Even more serious than the hard-core's poor education and lack of skills, says Leonard Nadler, a government consultant who also advises business on how to train these people, is "their attitude, characterized by tardiness and absenteeism, [which] betrays a great lack of understanding of what is expected of them in the world of work." What's needed to correct this attitude is "not only training that gives the person skills, but company procedures that help produce new behavior patterns and 'support' those patterns while he is undergoing training and also later while he is becoming adjusted to his job." According to Nadler, ". . . an additional element of attitude changing is related to appropriate dress and behavior on the job. The purpose is not to force conformity but rather to help the new employee understand the permissible range of dress on the job."[30]

Rules of proper dress, incidentally, are traditional ways of conditioning authoritarian behavior. The Eastman Kodak company, advertising its "career apparel" to business executives (which it refers to as a "euphemism for work uniforms"), makes clear the repressive nature of conformity in clothes. "The view from inside the uniform," says the ad, "serves as a reminder of obligation while wearing it, as distinguished from freedom as an individual human being when it is taken off."[31] That was an Eastman Kodak ad, mind you, not Herbert Marcuse.

According to Nadler, part of the "support systems" for producing new behavior patterns includes home visits. "Although the personnel or medical departments may become involved," he says, "the counselor should be called on for some of this work because of the trusting relationship he has established with the employee. But he must avoid *the appearance of* spying or invading privacy; if the new employee has been on welfare he has had enough of that."[32] (author's italics)

At General Motors, "marginal" workers are given this kind of "personal" treatment; but the techniques are somewhat less sophisticated. "If a worker fails to show up," said a *Fortune* article describing GM's "Project Opportunity," "one of a follow-up committee goes to the malingerer's house, hauls him out of bed, and delivers him to the factory; if the worker has personal problems, he is directed to agencies that help solve them."[33]

The educational content of these programs is geared directly to the jobs workers are to perform. Said Henry Ford II, describing his firm's "hardcore" programs during his campus lectures, "In routine jobs [which, one might imagine, Ford assembly plants supply in abundance], too much education may even be a handicap, and the man with less schooling may be a better risk." Yet Ford correctly senses that it is not simply higher pay that will get people to accept the conditions of their work. "More and more employees and potential employees are deciding that they would rather accept less pay for easier and pleasanter work," said Ford. "The cost of absenteeism and turnover is rising steeply, and it is increasingly difficult to maintain plant discipline." For Ford, whose lectures Yale President Kingman Brewster said reminded him of "that risk, and the gleeful willingness to take risk, [that] are essential to the capitalist promise" the problem resolves itself into one of more effective human management to ward off the impending result of discontent. "If management wants to get the most out of people, it will have to treat them as individuals," said Ford. "Twenty-three years ago in one of my first public speeches, I said that if business could learn to manage people as intelligently as it managed money and facilities, American industry would enter a new era. We still have a long way to go in that direction and we have to hurry, because the people *we manage* are getting more and more impatient."[34] (author's italics)

Dealing with "the individual" rather than a group has been industry's traditional method of attempting to avoid the potential threat of an organized effort of workers. In today's more scientifically oriented world, the workers' psychological motivations become the province for behavioral management by industry. Such problems of motivation are attributed to the worker's personal life rather than to his working conditions. For example, analyzing the problems of explaining to its present "motivated" workers why a firm is required to put up with excesses by blacks, the writer for *Fortune* states, "The malingering, of course, is the result of little experience in living by the clock, bad housing, and the dogmatic boredom that seems to afflict all the unmotivated."[35] Why "living by the clock" is a good way to live, why "good housing" should make tedious work attractive, and why anyone in his right mind should not be dogmatically bored at tedious work* is never touched on. Why

* An interesting analysis of the conditions created by capitalism comes from

93

should it be? It is hardly in the interest of business to use education as a means of motivating workers to understnd the repressive nature of their jobs. As Nadler says, their job is to "produce new behavior patterns," geared to the discipline required for efficient production—punctuality, proper dress and behavior. This behavior, of course, is defined by business, not by the workers themselves. As part of the motivation problem, the corporations must find ways to relieve boredom and the alienation that comes from the workers' lack of control over their own work—perhaps with more coffee breaks, perhaps softball games at lunchtime, perhaps approved courses in black history, or perhaps with

---

Lyndon B. Johnson, former U.S. President and a business entrepreneur himself.

. . . the capitalist is the man that, through prudence, accumulates wealth and takes that money and is willing to invest it. It may be to rebuild a whole new area. It may be to put skyscrapers in the sky. It may be to provide production lines for jobs. It may be to build railroads and dams. It can follow many lines. . . .

That manager is the fellow that gets up at daylight and works to midnight and develops stomach ulcers trying to get a bonus or trying to have a profit-sharing plan, or trying to build a better mousetrap at less cost, trying to compete not only with his fellowman here but with the rest of the world. . . .

Then the third segment there is the worker who gets to work at 8 and works to 5, and he has twenty-seven seconds to put the number of rivets in that car or that plane that he needs to. If he doesn't get them in in the twenty-seven seconds he goes to twenty-eight. That car or that plane moves on down the line—and it doesn't have the rivets in it! And you've wound up with a car that is missing a rivet a time or two yourselves. We all do that. But that poor fellow gets a coffee break twice a day. The rest of the time he has twenty-seven seconds to do that job and handle that machine.

He is the worker, and he hopes someday he can have a little hospital care, he can have a little pension, he can have a little social security, he can have a place to take Molly and the babies when he retires. That is his great love. His boys go to war, they fight to preserve this system. He likes his boss and he respects him. He believes in free enterprise, and he does not hate the man who makes a reasonable return.

Now those three—the capitalist, the manager, and the worker—make up free enterprise.

(From *Public Papers of the Presidents*, Lyndon B. Johnson, 1960–64, pp. 1, 147–51, in Gettleman, Marvin E., and Mermelstein, David, *The Great Society Reader*, Vintage Books, paperback, New York, 1967, pp. 125, 126.

"understanding" management who will take time to listen to their "gripes."

A meaningful education program for workers might at least pose ways in which work itself could be different in a humane society—might at least suggest that people have the right to do work that is personally satisfying so long as doing it doesn't involve the destruction of others (producing homes, for instance, instead of napalm). Automation, rather than being a threat to workers, could be used to eliminate the tedious work. Where automation wasn't possible, this kind of work could at least be shared equally among everyone in a community. Under our economic system automation is a threat to workers; along with their unions, workers fight to maintain their tedious, often mindless, jobs because losing their jobs means a degrading way of life—bad housing, bad education and the rest of the punishments our society inflicts on those who don't compete well. In a society which didn't make a job the passport for honorable existence, the workers themselves would be the first to insist on automation to get rid of tedious work; in many fields, full *unemployment* would become the goal.

The use of federal money for job-training programs is only a more recent effort in the history of government subsidy for social reforms which have benefited business. The initial wedge for this involvement came in the form of government housing programs as the result of the Depression in the Twenties and Thirties. These programs, as we will see, hardly began with the most radical segments of our society.

III

The Urban-Industrial Complex: PART TWO

GIVING IT MUSCLE: MONEY FROM WASHINGTON

AS LONG AS laissez-faire was profitable, the attitude of real-estate interests was to keep government out of the housing field. If the government built housing for the poor, argued Veiller, one of the most influential housing reformers of the early 1900s, then private developers would go out of business. "The only houses that will be built for the accommodation of the poor," he said, "will then be built by the city. . . . This can best be appreciated when it is understood that in the city of New York, for example, one hundred and twelve million dollars' worth of tenement houses were built during the year 1906."[1]

But the Depression of the Thirties was to change all this; there were no tenement developer's profits to protect when there was no money to develop tenements. Rather than a threat to private enterprise, government housing was seen as an opportunity. There would be profits for the private contractors who built the housing and the manufacturers who supplied the materials. Even the slum owner would profit indirectly by being able to extract more rent from the worker whose wages would increase through the government pump priming. In any case, with government as the only significant source of investment capital, private enterprise had little choice during the Thirties but to go along. It was a conservative President in 1931 who called for the "radical" public-housing program in this country.

Herbert Hoover's Conference on Home Building and Home Ownership suggested not only a public-housing program but the creation of a federal organization to provide reserve credit for home-financing institutions to get a better national distribution of mortgage money. While Hoover endorsed both recommendations and his administration established a number of government agencies to carry them out, it was Roosevelt who immersed the federal government in city housing problems on a massive scale. But Roosevelt was actually cool to the idea of the government becoming a real-estate developer. He and his New Dealers were primarily interested in government spending as a form of pump priming—putting up federal money to get the construction industry moving again. With not enough non-housing "public works" projects like bridges, roads and airports available, with the lengthy time necessary to produce such projects and with the relatively small labor force necessary to do the work, the housing some reformers were calling for became attractive.[2] Roosevelt's housing programs were not so much a conscious effort to house the "ill-housed," the "one third of a nation" of his famous 1936 inaugural address, as it was a convenient way to help industry put its own house in order. "FHA permitted builders to make fortunes without staking a penny of investment," wrote Charles Abrams, a well-known housing critic. Describing how government housing programs were geared not to helping the poor but rather to supporting the real-estate community, he said:

> The philosophy behind them was that the mortgage market was the mainstay of private building operations and that it was in the national interest to keep mortgage money

97

flowing even to the extent of pledging the full faith and credit of the federal government to mortgage lenders. With the same motivation, the federal government assured the savings and loan associations of liquidity, insured their depositors against loss, and bought up sour mortgages totaling more than three billion dollars from lending institutions.[3]

This federal program had its origin back in 1934, when the Federal Housing Administration was created to insure long-term, low-down-payment mortgages on new homes. The program's regulations, with specific recommendations which could be used to exclude financing for neighborhoods on the basis of the race, social characteristics and income of its occupants, effectively made the program one of government subsidies for more affluent and racially pure citizens. In evaluating neighborhoods for their "social characteristics," the 1938 federal manual stated:

> While the rating of this feature is based upon the group income characteristics of the occupant group at the immediate neighborhood of a location, other considerations, such as the varying social characteristics of neighborhood occupants, including the group attitude toward obligations and living standards, are warranted and will be reflected to some degree in the rating. By social characteristics are meant the moral qualities, the habits, the abilities and the social, educational and cultural backgrounds of the people residing in the immediate neighborhood.[4]

Not only did this "New Deal" agency require its underwriters to look at the potential neighborhood for investment but it also called for a similar investigation of areas close by:

> Areas surrounding a location are investigated to determine whether incompatible racial and social groups are present, for the purpose of making a prediction regarding the probability of the location being invaded by such groups. If a neighborhood is to retain stability, it is neces-

98

sary that properties shall continue to be occupied by the same social and racial classes. A change in social or racial occupancy generally contributes to instability and a decline in values.[5]

While discrimination through federal housing programs has been part of official government policy, at least one government official had taken even stronger measures. While running for the Vice Presidency in 1952, Richard M. Nixon was living in a house that he and his wife "protected" by co-executing an agreement to keep the house from ever being rented or sold to "any person or persons of Negro blood or extraction or to any person of the Semitic Race, blood or origin, which racial description shall be deemed to include Armenians, Jews, Hebrews, Persians and Syrians . . ."[6]

The discriminatory Federal Housing Administration regulations were being carried out as late as 1948.[7] But a year later, an even more effective way of exploiting the poor was to be found. In 1949, Congress passed a bill sponsored by the conservative Senator Robert Taft and the liberal Senator Robert Wagner. It was Title I of the act that allowed Washington to give the cities money to pay for condemning "blighted" private property, tear down buildings on it, then resell the land at a loss to real estate developers. It was this act that created urban renewal.

OPPORTUNITY KNOCKS

I submit that we have made a botch of urban renewal to date. By and large, people don't understand what we're after—or even what we're talking about. This is fortunate, for if they did, we'd all have to run for cover.

—David A. Wallace, former
director of the Philadelphia
Redevelopment Authority.[8]

With no Depression in the late Forties, the real-estate

developers had little interest in maintaining public-housing programs; what they could use, though, was more direct government subsidies of their own investments. Arguing against public housing, before Congress, Herbert U. Nelson, executive vice-president of the National Association of Real Estate Boards, asked instead for government help for his own community. "In our country," said Nelson, "we prefer that governmental activity shall take the form of assisting and aiding private business rather than undertaking great public projects of a governmental character."[9] In fact, he was actually describing government policy.

For many architects and planners, the government's urban-renewal programs promised the beginning of the millennium. There had long been the seed of large-scale projects in architectural theory, from the proposals of Antonio Sant Elia's Nuova Citta in 1910, Le Corbusier's Plan Voisin, Radiant City and Vertical City in the Twenties and Thirties to Buckminster Fuller's and Paolo Soleri's "megastructures" in the 1960s. The City Beautiful movement in the early 1900s gave many architects the brief hope that the American city could be transformed into a modern equivalent of ancient Rome. But such hopes were dashed as business kept city beautification to the minimum necessary level to appease the reformers.

Isolated projects such as New York's Rockefeller Center and the Radburn community in New Jersey were built, but the architects' visions remained on their drafting boards until the government stepped in to subsidize the construc-

Proposal by Le Corbusier, circa 1922

Co-op City, New York, 1968

tion and real-estate industries. With the coming of public housing, whole sections of cities could be torn down and replaced by towers of brick and glass. While some architects saw great hope in using the program to get rid of slums, for others it was a false start. Public housing was low-cost housing, and with it came a multitude of government design regulations to make sure the project buildings looked that way. After all, reasoned the real-estate interests, if the poor were living in better conditions than those who were supposed to be better off, what would happen to poor people's incentive to "work hard" so they could "live better"? Without "good" and "bad" housing, incentives would diminish, fewer people would put their earnings into housing, leaving the real-estate profit system in danger. In effect the program left little room for architectural muscle stretching; in the language of the profession, you couldn't do much about the "aesthetics." But with urban renewal more seemed possible; for the new clientele that would replace the poor, aesthetics and "culture" would be important. A book commissioned by the American Institute of Architects to commemorate its 100th anniversary summed up an important segment of professional attitudes:

> For the individuals with individuality the center might be a mecca if it could ever arise. But as it was, the central city was not rising in this form. Instead it was becoming a place for a few very rich people who sent their children

101

out of town to grow up, and a great many very poor who were far from urbane and would escape to the periphery as soon as their personal economics permitted. If they could be poured out of the central city and the non-suburbanites who lived in the suburbs be brought back to town there might yet be an elegant and urbane civilization in some American cities which would lift the level of the whole civilization.[10]

Hedging against the possible accusation of indifference to the plight of the poor rushing off to join the mass of dull conformists living in places other than the city center, liberals and planners called for the familiar remedy of "adequate relocation." Thus once making sure there was a program for adequately relocating the "individuals with individuality" in the city center, something would be done to compensate those who were "far from urbane," who happened to be living in the path of lifting the "level of the whole civilization."

But in reality even the sop of the government's relocation plan was farcical. While the 1949 urban-renewal legislation authorized construction of 810,000 public-housing units over a six-year period, by 1967, *eighteen* years later, only one

103

half the units had actually been built. But what had been accomplished under the banner of urban renewal, became a hard fact of life for many—400,000 homes, mostly those of lower-income people, were demolished in urban-renewal areas. In these areas only 107,000 housing units were built, with the result that for every four homes destroyed, only one was built. Yet even of those built, only 11,000, or less than *3 percent* of those destroyed, were public housing for poor people.

While these statistics don't include the housing not yet built but scheduled for construction, the projected figures show that at best only one housing unit would be built for every two destroyed. And of those to be built, the total number of "low and moderate income housing" would be 74,000, with most of these scheduled for people at the "upper ranges" of the moderate-income scale. Meanwhile, only 19,000 public-housing units for the poor, or less than *5 percent* of the total units that *have already been demolished,* are planned.[11]

In order to entice private developers, urban-renewal legislation allowed "fair value" of the sale price of a property to be set at considerably less than what the city actually paid to put the project together. With site preparation costs for urban renewal, like building demolition and legal negotiations for putting several smaller properties together in an attractive package, the city's cost for property acquisition can become quite high. To make up this loss, the federal government pays two thirds, with the city government picking up the remaining third.* In Boston, such subsidies allowed the city in one case to buy land at $7.40 per square foot, revalue it at $1.40 per square foot and then rent it to one of the mayor's political supporters at 6 percent of the new values. The land, once housing a low-income, pre-

---

* Through a system of federal credits to cities that make public improvements related to these projects—building streets and schools, for example—the city government's direct costs are usually a fraction or none of their one-third share, or approximately 14 percent.

dominantly Italian neighborhood, was later replaced with high-income apartment towers financed with government-insured loans. In New York City, private developers were replacing the poor with higher-income people, while being subsidized, in many cases, at the rate of $600,000 to $1 million an acre through urban-renewal funds.[12]

Besides the land-cost subsidy, developers can take advantage of one or more of a number of the federal government mortgage insurance programs to help finance their housing developments. Some programs where the developer is supposedly held to a limited return on investments require the developer to put up only a fraction of the total project costs, sometimes letting him do the project with no investment at all—what the developers call "mortgaging out." But the actual profit to the developer can be far in excess of the stipulated return since the federal housing laws provide for such allowances as rapid depreciation, "packaging fees," management fees and construction profits. Additionally, in many states, cities could use real-estate tax abatements as a way of attracting developers.

With government control of urban renewal, the planners could achieve more centralized control of design decisions. Since many equated orderliness, wholeness and unity with beauty, a perfect marriage could be made—centralized decisions to achieve uniformity in design. In 1959 the American Institute of Planners' policy statement on urban renewal said, "Renewal offers an opportunity to secure superior urban design when relatively large areas of land are improved under coordinated design leadership and relatively uniform site and building controls.[13]

As more money was pumped into urban renewal, more architects began to design projects involving not only one or a few buildings but often whole complexes of buildings. The title "architect," no longer appropriate because of its traditional connotation with single-building design, had to be changed. Many architects became "urban designers" and

105

"city planners" overnight, investing themselves with the proper credentials for their new role.

TOMORROW THE WORLD

As urban designer the architect sees himself as the man who dictated the design for the entire built environment. Such megalomania had strong support from the leaders in the field. Said the president of the American Institute of Architects:

> The total environment produced by architecture in the next 40 years can become greater than the Golden Age of Greece, surpass the glory of Rome and outshine the magnificence of the Renaissance. Such an end is possible provided the architect assumes again his historic role as Master Builder. In such a role, he must retain the basic control not only of individual buildings, but of all design involved with man-made environment.[14]

To which the president of the American Institute of Planners added:

> The greatest service the American Institute of Architects could render would be to develop the essential outlines of a curriculum for the continuing education of the architect, the Master Builder of the total environment by whatever name we call him.[15]

The AIP president went on to suggest that architects should come together in workshops throughout the country "to evolve the approach to planning solutions adequate to meet the needs of cities of all sizes and the needs of the total environment of city and country, not only in America, but in all nations of the world."[16]

Such "megavisions" by the planners might be written off as artistic fantasies were it not that liberal reformers bent on "good design" helped such concepts flourish, as did the more conservative business interests willing to buy them off for the pot of gold at the end of the urban-renewal rainbow.

What all three—the liberal, the conservative and the planner—were headed for was centralized control of city development. According to the views of John Burchard and Albert Bush-Brown, the two architectural historians commissioned by the American Institute of Architects to write their 100-year history:

> Major civic surgery was needed, surgery and grafting; fantastic cooperation between financial powers; brilliant new political machinery and courageous and foresighted politicians; in the end it surely meant abandonment of much private interest in favor of a greater and communal urban interest.[17]

In the end what it surely meant was abandoning some private interest, but the interests served were other, more powerful, private ones—the real-estate developers, surely not those who were displaced to other filthy conditions or the small homeowner and small businessman. The "brilliant new political machinery" that was urban renewal paved the way for bigger government subsidies for the entrepreneurs. And "communal urban interest" was the euphemism for central control by business, government and the planners, removing political power from the groups that were to be displaced.

Surgery, grafting—that was the planners' pseudo-science in the service of the cultural and economic prejudices of those controlling urban renewal. To rationalize a program of removing the poor for the benefit of business, the disease metaphor was marched out: the city was sick and had to be cured. Using medical metaphors gives the sense of organic phenomena. The city as a body operates well, but now and then has some aberrations—some cancers. Cut out the cancers, goes the argument, and the body will continue its proper functioning.

A report by the University of Pennsylvania's Institute for Urban Studies is another revealing example of urban pseudo-science in action. Asked by the Philadelphia Redevelopment

107

Authority to find "the demand for housing" in a downtown area, university experts displayed quantities of objective-sounding analysis and data, including such tables as "Median Ratio of Gross Rent to Income by Income Class, Families and Primary Individuals Living in Households, Philadelphia Standard Metropolitan Area, 1950 and 1956."[18] Then at the close of the report comes the professionals' real bias about whom the city is being rebuilt for and whose demand is going to be met:

> . . . the persons who are presently in the area and those who will be attracted to it are eminently equipped to produce the type of community leadership necessary to sustain a large metropolis. They are educated, have high incomes, are mature and not burdened with the financial and time costs of rearing young children. They, therefore, are free to devote a substantial portion of their leisure hours to the support of the arts and of various community activities.[19]

From that description it is clear that the professionals writing the report had omitted many of the people living in the core area at the time as potential residents after urban renewal. In fact, although never stated in the report, the poor are obviously the ones who will be "asked" to leave—i.e., those who in the eyes of the professionals are not "eminently equipped to produce the type of community leadership necessary to sustain a large metropolis"; those who are *not* educated; those who do *not* have high incomes; those who in their eyes are *not* "mature"; those who *are* burdened with the financial and time costs of rearing young children; and those who do *not* support the kind of arts and "various community activities" the professionals would like to see supported.

With similar reasoning, business has used renewal to flush out the poor and make areas attractive for more lucrative tenants. "As Alcoa's redevelopment projects come on-stream," said Leon E. Hickman, Alcoa's vice-president in charge of real estate, "we see the battle line forming in every instance." Hickman, whose company also has substantial investments in urban-renewal projects, continued, "On one side of the street stands our development—new, prideful, and hopeful. On the other side of the street—too often literally—stand the slums, waiting to take us over." Calling for continued government planning and money for urban renewal, Hickman warned that little would come of redevelopment if government and the private sector are "not organized to clean out the remaining blight. Otherwise it is too much like removing part of a cancer."[20]

By 1963, over 60 percent of the people being removed along with the "cancers" were black people, Puerto Ricans and other minority groups.[21] And lest renewal agencies be accused of practicing racism, "black face" techniques were developed by planners to show that everybody was getting the same bad deal. "I was in charge of relocation and my assistant was a colored woman," said one renewal-agency relocation officer. "She's now supervisor of relocation. We had the same office, desk to desk. It helped show people we weren't using urban renewal for Negro removal."[22]

HIGHWAY GRAVY TRAIN

Secretary of Commerce Hodges in a recent issue of the *American Weekly* warned of the increasing threat of restrictions on motor vehicles. Hitting the nail squarely on the head, Secretary Hodges pointed out that "traffic problems will not be mastered by removing cars from our roads, but by providing better roads and more, not less, accommodations for cars." We shout a "Hear, hear!" and let's construct those better roads of asphalt so they will cost less to build and thus be easy on taxes—at the same time providing more roads for more cars to travel more miles and use more petroleum products. This is basic to travel development.

—*Asphalt Institute Quarterly*[23]

109

To make the "urban crisis" attractive to the large corporations, a guaranteed market for urban-crisis products is
required—a market that won't get uppity and politically
embarrassing about what gets produced. Besides a mass,
docile and receptive market, the corporation would like government subsidies that aren't subject to the yearly whims of
political representatives. Urban renewal and government
housing programs, as yet, haven't qualified for these kinds
of "major league" operations. With the exceptions of companies like Alcoa and Reynolds Aluminum, clients of these
programs are traditionally large real-estate developers. By
contrast, Washington's ventures in helping states build
highways have been a "natural" operation for the larger
industrial corporations. The reason lies at least partially in
the difference between urban real-estate development and
the nature of what the large industrial corporation
produces.

Making a housing unit involves dealing with local build-

110

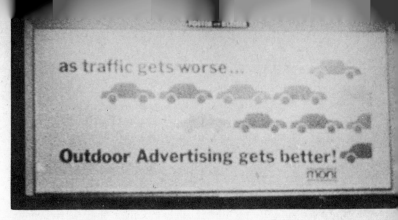

as traffic gets worse...

Outdoor Advertising gets better!

ing codes, local construction unions, local politicians and local political problems such as racial integration and black power. Urban renewal, for example, has generated bitter political controversies—especially as those whose lives have been uprooted have grown more militant in rejecting the planners' designs. Until recently the highway builders had a relatively free hand—in part because most highways were built outside the cities, but also because highways are built by state agencies, which are traditionally less sensitive to local politics than are city agencies.

Moreover, cars and oil, as products, give the corporations a more clearly defined view of their market—and control over their products—than a housing unit. The product is usually finished when it leaves the factory. The exception of recent state and federal regulations on safety and pollution

control devices on autos, and the growing controversies over the lead content in gasoline, are relatively simple problems for the corporations compared with having to deal with a myriad of city and federal agencies and "actors" involved with housing development.

Although such corporations as Alcoa and Reynolds Aluminum became big real-estate developers using urban renewal and other programs, they are more the exceptions than the rule. Being aluminum companies, they were largely interested in providing a demand for their aluminum building products through their own real-estate development. At the same time, Alcoa's original involvement was through a partnership with William Zeckendorf, a well-known real-estate developer. When Zeckendorf got into trouble by over-extending his real-estate speculation, Alcoa bought out Zeckendorf's share of the projects. For the most part, large real-estate developers with political contacts in the cities in which they operate, rather than industrial corporations, have been the traditional clients of government renewal and housing programs. They have become the skilled practitioners in manipulating government real-estate programs and in weathering political controversies which have sometimes surrounded their development.

It is not without reason, then, that Washington's urban renewal and housing programs, although a boon to real-estate developers, have been minor by comparison with its highway programs. The Interstate Highway System, signed into law by President Dwight D. Eisenhower, was recently described by John A. Volpe, head of the Department of Transportation and a former highway contractor, as "the biggest public works project in the history of the world."*[24] That Washington's spending to help states build highways is one of its most expensive budget items is hardly unrelated

* In addition to building highways, the Transportation Secretary was once president of the Associated General Contractors of America. The new Department of Transportation building was built, incidentally, by his former firm—the John A. Volpe Company—which is now run by his brother.

to the fact that seven of the country's ten largest corporations produce either oil or cars,[25] and twenty of the thirty-five wealthiest people have gained their abundance from the same kind of production.[26] In addition, the biggest single market for steel in this country is connected with highways; one fifth of all the steel produced is used for either cars or highway construction.[27]

After Eisenhower had proposed that the federal government spend $50 billion on highways back in July 1954, he decided it would be useful to set up a committee to study specific highway needs—a little bit of the horse-behind-the cart philosophy if you really believed that the major purpose of building highways was to improve transportation. "The automobile has restored a way of life in which the individual may live in a friendly neighborhood," concluded the study committee, "it has brought city and country closer together, it has made us one country and a united people. But, America continues to grow. Our highway plant must similarly grow if we are to maintain and increase our standard of living."[28] These conclusions aren't much of a surprise when you consider the men who made up the committee. Headed by businessman Lucius D. Clay, a former general who was then Continental Can's chairman of the board, it consisted of David Beck, International Brotherhood of Teamsters president (who represented truck drivers and was later convicted of tampering with their pension funds); S. Sloan Colt, president of Bankers Trust Company; William A. Roberts, Allis-Chalmers president (road-building-equipment manufacturer); and Stephen D. Bechtel, president of the Bechtel Construction Corporation (large public-works projects). Bechtel, whose stated worth is between $100 and $200 million, is the ninth richest man in the United States.[29]

So strong are the business interests guiding Washington's highway programs that when Congress called for a $6 billion cut in government spending in 1968 in order to continue

113

the blood bath in Vietnam, its $12.3 billion 1968 Highway
Act added still more mileage to the highway program. And
the year before, while Congress was cutting its poverty
funds by $300 million, its new Model Cities program by
$350 million and its meager $40 million rent supplement to
$10 million, an attempt to cut back highway money was
quickly defeated.[30] The experience of the highway programs, like urban renewal, is another frightening forecast
of what to expect when business, government and the planners are marshaled to solve urban problems.

The $56 billion Interstate Highway System, a major part
of the federal government's road-building effort, will use 45
percent of its funds in urban areas.[31] This system alone,
supported by gasoline taxes which go into a "trust fund,"
provides the natural climate for the large corporations to
thrive in. The trust fund, putting four cents for every gallon
of gasoline sold into a kitty which can be used only to build
highways, provides an ever-increasing fund divorced from
yearly Congressional appropriations. This subsidy, running
at the rate of $4 billion a year, gives the states a ninety-cent
subsidy for every ten cents they spend to build the Interstate. This "90–10" formula makes for an irresistible inducement for states to build highways almost anywhere just
to get their hands on the subsidy.

"Highway officials," says the Asphalt Institute, a "non-
profit" propaganda arm of the petroleum industry, "are not
merely spenders of the taxpayers' money. They are managers of huge revenue-producing transportation systems."
The Institutute's *Quarterly* continues:

> Every new mile tacked onto the paved road and street
> system is accompanied by the consumption of about 50,000
> additional gallons of motor fuel a year. That's a total of
> $2\frac{1}{4}$ billion additional gallons of fuel use, accounted for
> solely by the added 45,000 paved miles (the amount of new
> roads and streets built each year). . . . In short, we have
> a self-perpetuating cycle, the key element of which is new

114

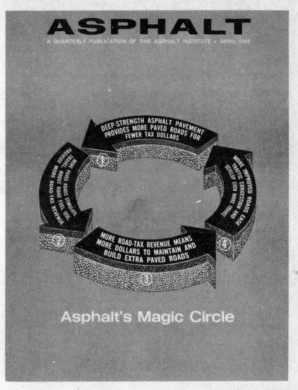

ASPHALT

A QUARTERLY PUBLICATION OF THE ASPHALT INSTITUTE · APRIL 1966

DEEP-STRENGTH ASPHALT PAVEMENT PROVIDES MORE PAVED ROADS FOR FEWER TAX DOLLARS

MORE IMPROVED ROADS EASE TRAFFIC CONGESTION AND DEVELOP EVEN MORE TRAVEL

MORE PAVED ROADS STIMULATE TRAVEL, BOOST ROAD FUEL USE, MORE ROAD-TAX REVENUE

MORE ROAD-TAX REVENUE MEANS MORE DOLLARS TO MAINTAIN AND BUILD EXTRA PAVED ROADS

Asphalt's Magic Circle

paved roads. The 45,000 new miles added to the road and street network each year accommodate automotive travel, generate fuel consumption, produce road-building revenue. Scratch the new roads and the cycle ceases to function. Three million new vehicles surging into the traffic stream each year without new paved mileage to provide necessary running room: the spectacle is too miserable to contemplate.[32]

Apparently what's not too difficult for the Asphalt Institute to contemplate is the idea that people ought to be induced to drive longer distances in order to get people to use more gas and provide money to build more roads.

115

Elevated highway of today

Elevated railroad of the late 1800s

It is the purpose of travel development to encourage motorists to take more pleasure and vacation trips and drive longer distances. . . . If the campaign is successful, it will automatically effect a rise in annual fuel consumption per vehicle and thus make more revenue available for road construction.[33]

A few years ago, as part of a planning group working with neighborhood groups against the proposed construction of Boston's highway system, I went to see the transportation editor of a "liberal" Boston newspaper. We told the editor about the social disaster that would follow the proposed system, causing the displacement in one small city alone of 1,500 families (5 percent of the city's total population), the loss of over 2,000 jobs and the removal of one of the few long-time racially mixed neighborhoods in the Boston area. "Well, it may not be the best system," he told us after we argued for designing a more integrated transit and highway system, "but we've studied the road to death, and you just have to realize the state could use the money." Considering Washington's enormous contribution to state economies through its 90 percent underwriting of state highway building, it shouldn't be very surprising that the states will build almost anything to bring home the federal largess. Thus the highway lobby, through its influence on centralized federal programs, affects what are legally decentralized perogatives of the states.

Since funds for the federal Interstate Highway System are collected by a gas tax on those who drive, rather than a general tax on the public, it is often argued that the motorist is paying his way—what's called a "user tax." That is, every time a motorist buys a gallon of gas he pays four cents into the trust fund, and by so doing he supposedly decides that building more highways is the right thing to do. The argument obviously forgets that while highways' users may pay the financial cost of constructing the highways, they don't pay for the disruption of neighborhoods and lives by these

highways. And is the motorist really making a conscious choice to build highways by paying four cents for every gallon of gasoline he buys—or isn't it rather that he has few alternatives if he wants to get from one place to another? He is not asked, for example, if he wants his user tax to be spent on building mass transit rather than highways. He hasn't the choice, for example, of having his tax pay to improve and make safe existing highways and local street systems by building, say, underpasses and better traffic lighting instead of inducing people to drive more by building more highways.

But even in traditional economic terms, the user-tax argument is nonsense. If a road is built, there are many secondary effects the user doesn't pay for. The road generates the need for parking garages, which are paid for by the city. Additional air pollution caused by the new facilities means costs for medical bills and antipollution control that are not paid by the user. Reduced use of transit caused by new roads means higher fares and larger public sudsidies for the transit companies, which again aren't paid for by the trust-fund user taxes.

GOD, SALVATION AND HIGHWAYS

O Almighty God, who has given us this earth and has appointed men to have domination over it; who has commanded us to make straight the highways, to lift up the valleys and to make the mountains low, we ask thy bless-

ing upon these men who do just that. Fill them with a
sense of accomplishment, not just for the roads built, but
for the ways opened for the lengthening of visions, the
broader hopes and the greater joys which makes these
highways a possibility for mankind.

Bless these, our Nation's road builders, and their
friends. For the benefits we reap from their labors, we
praise thee; may thy glory be revealed in us. Amen.

—"Prayer for America's Road
Builders"—official prayer
of the American Road Builders'
Association[34]

Today, 60 percent of the total air pollution in most U.S.
cities is caused by auto exhaust. Each day in Los Angeles,
which supposedly has some of the most progressive legislation against air pollution in the country, 80 percent of the
city's air pollution—12,000 tons of pollutants—is pumped
into the air by automobiles. Almost every other day in that
city public-school children aren't allowed to exercise because
of the amount of breathing it would take, while a group of
sixty UCLA medical faculty suggested that people without

special reasons for being in that city should leave.[35] By 1975, an ecological study recently warned, the "air pollution in the [Los Angeles] basin will be at levels where mass mortality can be expected."[36]

The auto death rates are already an entrenched part of Americana. Each year more than 50,000 people are killed in auto accidents, or one person every eleven minutes. But in the face of these morbid conditions, a representative of the highway corporations' lobby can, in all seriousness, tell us that the *only* way to redevelop our cities is to build more highways. "These highway networks are the only available method—let me repeat," said Harry A. Williams, director of the Automobile Manufacturers Association, "the *only* available method—for redeveloping those parts of our central cities which have become blighted or will become blighted in coming years. Such freeways, coupled with major arterial routes feeding into them, create neighborhood cells within which the city planner can work with confidence in redeveloping neighborhoods that have become structurally or functionally obsolete.[37]

Another representative of the highway corporations can, again in all seriousness, invoke "beauty" as the cause for building more roads. According to Mr. H. E. Humphreys, former president of United States Rubber Company:

> If our generation and succeeding ones become—as seems likely—more and more conscious of beauty, it will be because every road that is built can and should make more beauty accessible to more people. In a year's time, a few hundred people may be able to afford the time and the energy to *hike* through a woods or a park. But every day, hundreds of *thousands* may drive through those woods and parks, when carefully designed highways unfurl the whole, lovely view.[38]

Why should people bother walking through the woods, goes his argument, when they can behold its beauty from behind the steering wheels of their cars (all with four rubber tires that are wearing out in the cause of more and more people becoming conscious of beauty) ? Why should they even strain themselves driving through the woods on superhighways when, by the same argument, they could duplicate the experience of that woods at a movie. (I expect we'll have to wait until the United States Rubber Company starts making films before we get that analysis of bringing beauty to the masses.)

But if you happen to be a sports fan instead of a nature lover, the Federal Highway Administration, Washington's agency in charge of the program, has this equally sophisticated highway-building rationale for you. "The budding basketball star of tomorrow," says the agency, "could be a kid who learned how to dribble, pass, and shoot because an Interstate Highway came through his neighborhood. And this same youth, who wiled away hours of his life wondering what to do next, can now cavort on a basketball court laid out under a structurally modern viaduct."[39]

These obviously self-serving suggestions may seem to approach the limits of absurdity, but they're hardly very far from those of the more "rational" planning experts. With the visual and social results of the highway system becoming more and more apparent (especially to those threatened with displacement) many communities have organized themselves to stop the onslaught. To combat this politically embarrassing opposition, the government has developed sophisticated pacification programs. As Francis C. Turner, Federal Highway Administrator, put it, "Now we have to change people's minds and sell them on a relocation plan." "Before," continued Turner, "we just bought property and relocation was their [the states'] responsibility."[40] Instead of simply designing a highway and ramming it down the community's throat, "interdisciplinary teams" of experts, often including "community representatives," are now put together to find soothing alternatives.

One proposal, the work of architect Archibald C. Rogers,

121

for a "design concept team" of architects, city planners, engineers and sociologists to help with a controversial highway in Baltimore, was quickly adapted as a model for other cities by the Department of Transportation. According to Rogers, the team is founded on the idea that "we are capable of creating today major engineering works, such as an Urban Freeway System, that can become beautiful public monuments enhancing the city in which they are built."[41] In Baltimore, the local American Institute of Architects chapter decided against joining an attack being made against building a highway; instead, Rogers and a group of "top architects" argued that with local leaders, the highways could be a force to "reform and revitalize the city."[42] The approach, which was to include work with local community groups, was put to work in that city under a $4.8 million contract to a design concept team, including Skidmore, Owings and Merrill, the largest architectural firm in the country. When a black neighborhood group decided it didn't want the road at all, the team was told by Joseph Axelrod, chief of the Interstate Division of the State Roads for Baltimore, to stop its work with the community.[43] Although the team went on to patch up some of the worst effects of the original design, the basic decision—about whether or not the road should be built at all—was obviously ordained by the rules of the game. Meanwhile, the design concept team picked up another $4.7 million contract for more work in Baltimore.

The universities provide another convenient ground for gathering planning mandarins to rationalize these roads. In the tradition of government-sponsored university work, the research doesn't involve questioning policy assumptions; for example, it doesn't ask whether or not the Interstate Highway program itself really is in the interest of developing humane environments. Similarly, in cold-war research, the government sponsors no university work that questions America's involvement in counter-revolutions. What it does supply is research funds for expert rationalizations and techniques to deliver its programs, and that's what gets produced. At MIT, for example, a research project financed by Washington's Bureau of Public Roads was supposedly aimed at developing techniques of making highways responsive to local needs. In fact, the research was geared to making sure the highways get built. According to the MIT report, their study "will reduce the number and intensity of costly and divisive highway controversies, will provide more attractive roads, will improve the urban environment and will *help insure the continuance of the highway construction program.*" (author's italics) To do this, the report says, the job of those in charge of planning highway locations is "in general helping to generate enough positive impact to get the community behind the highway proposal instead of opposed to it." Using the same logic as the highway lobbyists and Rogers' design concept team, which never questions the basic rationale for building highways, the highway becomes an opportunity for community development. "Instead of being seen in a negative light, as something to be blocked," the report suggests, "the highway should be used as a driving force capable of catalyzing a broad range of physical, social, and economic improvements. . . ."[44]

A conference of architects and highway officials, including the head of the American Institute of Architects, developed a similar approach. Supposedly concerning itself with "the impact of the highway upon people" and "the aesthetic fabric of the urban area," the conference's conclusions strangely raise not even the slightest suggestion that people or the "aesthetic fabric of the urban area" might in some cases be better off without the construction of highways. Rather, "[t]he construction of freeways on the scale now planned during this period of rapid change and growth will provide unprecedented opportunities to help shape and structure the urban community in a manner which meets the needs of people who live, work and travel in these areas."[45]

For the kind of physical improvements the highway systems are supposed to generate, highway builders can select from a range of the planners' "urban design" theories. The theories, often embellished in the language of aesthetic metaphors, like those which will be described in Chapter IV, are attractive to middle-class, "cultured" interests. Issues are dealt with in aesthetic terms, like Rogers' description of freeways as "beautiful public monuments." Or according to Charles W. Moore, chairman of Yale's School of Architecture, "[t]he freeways could be the real monuments of the future, the places set aside for special celebration by people able to experience space and light and motion and relationships to other people and things at a speed that so far only this century has allowed."[46] Using this acceptable currency, the planner doesn't seem to be making the political value judgments which are an inevitable part of his work. Instead, his work is made to seem self-evident as a proper thing to do. Not everyone will agree on what is beautiful, but most will agree that things should be beautiful. Therefore, on with the work.

THE CORPORATE CRYSTAL BALL

With the growing intrusion of urban renewal and highways into urban areas being opposed by an increasingly militant segment of the population, an urban-industrial complex can no longer count on the docile, receptive market it needs to continue its smooth operations. In the Boston area, for example, the entire $400 million highway system has been held up for years by a coalition of neighborhood groups. Similar anti-urban renewal and anti-highway efforts in other parts of the country, notably Washington, D.C., San Francisco, New Orleans and New York, have posed similar threats to traditional urban imperialism.

All this isn't to say industry is about to lie down and play dead. In the case of highways, the corporations will likely support liberal pacification programs in urban areas, such as paying higher relocation costs, building housing over highways and building "more beautiful" highways. To keep the federal money flowing they will also attempt to focus more on building rural and suburban highways, where the political opposition is not so strong as in central-city areas.

Business can rightfully claim that their primary responsibility in a corporate free-enterprise system is to make a profit for their stockholders—not that they would be against solving social problems if that was consistent with their "enlightened self-interest." Government, on the other hand, is looked to by massive numbers of its constituents as the primary solver of social problems. Since government's real role, in effect, has come to be protector of corporate interests under a mandate to solve social problems, it seeks solutions which can do both. The result has been to subsidize corporations through programs of social welfare. As Senator Robert F. Kennedy once told a group of building-products manufacturers, "We in government can help you by providing the incentives and protection for the uncertainty of investing in these neglected neighborhoods." Calling for private industry to invest in the ghettos, on another occasion he noted that "private enterprise will require incentives, credits, accelerated depreciation, and extra deductions as effective and as comprehensive as those that we now offer for the production of oil or the building of grain storage facilities, or the supersonic transport."[47]

But to provide such inducements, political representatives must also be able to get their constituents to pay for welfare programs, like housing, education and job training for the poor, mass transit, etc. While the government was able to muster a liberal-conservative consensus on the cold war, it looks increasingly doubtful that this is possible on the urban crisis. For some, "law and order" is the way to deal with the problem; for others it is "welfare programs." Some believe in centralized education, others in decentralized education;

some in integrated education, others in community-controlled education. Some believe in housing the poor in suburbs; others want it in the central city. Some are in favor of industrialized housing; others, especially the construction unions, will probably oppose it. For some, training blacks for jobs means their own jobs are threatened.

When people feel their lives are being threatened by hoards of enemies working day and night to destroy them, it is not so difficult for them to see the single answer of military protection. But when they are confronted with problems on a more personal day-to-day basis—when it's their kids being bussed to a decrepit ghetto school, or their problem of finding a job because of racist attitudes and bad education—then there is likely to be intense local opposition to some government programs.

To avoid clots in the federal money flow resulting from such clashes, business will likely propose the creation of government super-agencies with centralized powers, free from the vagaries of local political control. These agencies will move toward the same kinds of ties with industry that have worked so well with NASA and the Pentagon. "The question is," according to *Business Week*, "how soon the demand for better housing, transportation, medical care, and the rest can be translated into the real markets needed to gain industry's commitment. As yet, no monied monolith like the Defense Department has arisen to define and finance the new goals."[48]

A writer for *Fortune*, another magazine aimed at corporate policy-makers, laments, "No single agency—or single purpose—guides the urban program, as NASA does in space or the Pentagon in weaponry. The major problem therefore is to find some profit-oriented mechanism by which the great talents of systems-oriented industry can be brought to bear on the great needs of the cities."[49] If anyone ever stood in need of an argument that the free-enterprise system is dead in this country and that government is a mechanism to

126

promote the corporation's profit, he can find much in the last two statements in these journals of the free and enterprising. What we are told is that the demand side of the supply-and-demand equation is to be a function of govenment and not demand. What is needed is a government "monolith" like NASA or the Pentagon to "translate" demands into markets, or to "find some profit-oriented mechanism" to stimulate "the great talents of systems-oriented industry." If there are demands, why must they be translated? If there are demands, then why does government have to find some profit-oriented mechanism (which I take as the euphemism for subsidies) to stimulate business? Isn't business's supply under capitalist economics supposed to equal the demand?

Business Week goes on to examine an optimistic future. "Over the next ten years," it predicts, "federal revenue sharing with local government or some similar programs will probably release enough money for cities and states to hire companies for civilian projects, much as companies do now for the Defense Department or NASA."[50] A similar approach is suggested by Kenneth Andrews of the Harvard

127

Business School. He sees organizations like Comsat taking over such large civilian projects as schools and hospitals.[51] The models to which business is looking are either existing centralized agencies or new ones with which they can jointly determine urban priorities and then have the central agencies contract with them to help solve the "urban crisis."

A recently created public corporation to promote statewide urban renewal in New York State gives some further insights into what to expect from centralized government agencies working with business to solve the urban crisis. The purpose of the organization, called the Urban Development Corporation (UDC), was clearly stated in an article in one of the professional architectural magazines. "It is apparent," said the author, "the private developers are just not going to wade into the swampy waters of the cities without having someone else wade in and cut a clear channel through the swamp."[52] Indeed, the state couldn't have picked a more formidable "swamp wading" combination than Edward J. Logue and the organization he formulated and now heads. The UDC, funded by a billion dollars in state bonds, has virtual immunity from local controls; it can condemn property, override local zoning and building codes and plan, build, manage and promote its own projects. As yet the organization can't sell property to private developers at a loss to itself; but, says one sympathetic reporter who agrees with Logue's "doer" approach, he and his planners are working on that "defect."[53] According to the same source, Logue, who rose to fame as chief of two of the country's biggest urban-renewal programs—in New Haven and Boston —sees the role of his government-supported agency as tied to the interest of business. "Uncomfortable with community-action people," says the reporter, "dismayed by the average, time-serving public official, Logue fits in well with business people. The UDC doesn't make a move without elaborately consulting with them and, often . . . getting them to put up some money to match UDC's financial commitment to a

128

project or plan." As for city participation in the project, the UDC allows it to the extent necessary to retain its power.

The UDC gave one city, for example, the right to reject its development plans or developers, while at the same time giving itself the right to walk out on a project if it didn't like what the local people were doing. With UDC holding powerful financial cards, most cities have little choice but to go along. "What a city gets from UDC in return for sacrificing some of its traditional prerogatives," says this reporter, "is a very fair compensation—expertise and economic resources it could not otherwise command, not to mention, when a project is finished, tax-producing structures. One could say that the autonomy surrendered is roughly akin to that which a sick man gives up to a hospital. It may be annoying, but it does offer the possibility of curing what ails him."[54] There are those medical metaphors again, and Logue, being an "expert" on city planning matters, naturally marched his programs under the familiar banner of the urban medic. "Locally, cities must take slums seriously," he wrote in 1958 when he was urban-renewal chief in Boston, "and recognize them for the cancers they are. Cities must organize themselves to fight slums as efficiently and matter-of-factly as they now organize to fight fires."[55]

Logue's fire-fighting and cancer cures are his euphemisms for removing the poor to redevelop central-city areas for a more affluent clientele. "Our approach is to renew the neighborhoods for the people who now live in them," claimed Logue during the early 1960s. But in fact his renewal programs were forcing people out of their neighborhoods. In one area, Logue's redevelopment program stated in 1966, "that provision would be made under the plan for housing all low-income families and individuals desiring to remain in this community."[56] But by early 1968, 251 families had been displaced from this neighborhood by the renewal agency.[57] In other cases where new housing was provided, increased rents effectively stopped poor residents from tak-

129

ing advantage of programs that were supposedly improving *their* neighborhoods.

Logue's cancer and fire-fighting programs are not surprisingly tied to where private developers can make money. Thus his self-tailored Urban Development Corporation can do all its own financing, *except* to subsidize low-income housing. For this it must rely on traditional government programs, which obviously aren't in abundant supply. So the UDC is "forced" to turn its attention and its expertise to more profitable projects. On top of this, Logue's "formula" limiting low-income housing to 20 percent in those UDC projects where it actually is provided effectively gives the agency the role of packaging lucrative programs for private developers.

The UDC is simply one example of the direction the urban industrial complex will take in the future. A myriad of other "urban crisis" models are being developed by business and government. In California, for example, the Ford Motor Company is developing a "comprehensive" transportation system for San Diego County, while Space-General, a subsidiary of the Aerojet-General Corporation, has been investigating that state's welfare system, its courts, its penal institutions, and its police departments.

I have already described business's outright involvement in adopting public schools in Connecticut and Michigan or training public-school students in other states. The traditional conduct of private programs masquerading as public improvements, although still quite useful, is becoming less necessary for the corporations. As government continues to fail in solving the urban crisis, not only does the call for "efficient," "no-nonsense" solutions by private enterprise become more acceptable, but liberal sentiment turns toward the view that, as Robert F. Kennedy said, government should provide the "incentives," the "protection" for such solutions. In effect, those who pay the bulk of the taxes, the poor and the middle class, are being asked to pay those who cause the crisis to provide the solutions for this very same crisis. Yet even such solutions, as we have seen in the cases of urban renewal, housing, transportation, education, and job-training programs, far from creating the humane society which would replace the urban crisis, has only served to further the nature of the existing society; people are being asked to finance their own repression.

Now that the poor and many of the middle class have become increasingly hostile to such efforts, there is a real need and climate for radical change. The problem then would seem one of moving toward a new political and economic framework which could allow this to happen. Yet such a "system," which I discuss later in this book, is only a partial answer. We must first be able to recognize that our political and economic system not only distorts our political and economic actions but does this to many of our other cultural forms. Herbert Marcuse posed this problem when he described revolutionary political change in the context of changing the language of a culture. "It has been said that the degree to which a revolution is developing *qualitatively* different social conditions and relationships," he wrote, "may perhaps be indicated by the development of a different language: the rupture with the continuum of domination must also be a rupture with the vocabulary of domination."[58]

As an architect, I find Marcuse's "vocabulary of domination" applies as well to the way we approach designing our environment. We don't have to look very far for examples of this. As you will see, we either live in them already or, if some of the better known planners have their way, we soon will.

131

IV

The Architecture
of Repression

As an architect, if I had no economic or social limitations, I'd solve all my problems with one-story buildings. Imagine how pleasant it would be to always work and plan in spaces overlooking lovely gardens filled with flowers.

Yet, we know that within the framework of our present cities this is impossible to achieve. Why? Because we must recognize social and economic limitations and requirements. A solution without such recognition would be meaningless.[1]

—Minoru Yamasaki, an architect for the Pruitt-Igoe
Public Housing Project in St. Louis

Pruitt-Igoe Public Housing Project, St. Louis

THE GRAND CENTRAL STATION area in New York City is one of the most congested business districts in the world. It seethes with the congestion caused by real-estate speculation, the subways are jammed, and few rays of sunshine ever make it to the nearly impassable streets. In 1968 Marcel Breuer, a "world-renowned" architect, designed a 55-story 2,000,000-square-foot building to be perched on top of the existing Grand Central structure. Coincidentally, a week after the design was presented, Breuer received the Gold Medal of the American Institute of Architects, its highest award.

In some ways, Breuer's design is not so absurd as it may seem. Our economic system has traditionally reduced the architect (the planner as environmental designer) to the role of providing culturally acceptable rationalizations for projects whose form and use have already been determined by real-estate speculation. The developers who build these projects must contend with a large segment of the population with sensitive bourgeois attitudes about culture—attitudes which have been conditioned by their contact with Western aesthetic models. But these are projects whose goals have nothing to do with the aesthetics of a humane existence.

In the case of the Grand Central project, the air rights over the terminal building were worth $60 million. With that kind of value, the need to build something, or rather anything, to reap the potential profit of the site seems obvious. And what of the architectural concepts in such a project? Are they relevant to the way people live in the congested area, what it's like to work in the anonymous offices, or to walk on the sunless streets? According to Breuer, his prime concern was to make the new building a "calm background" for the façade of the terminal.[2] Nowhere in the language of formal values does one feel the pressures of the building's prospective effect on the adjacent area. Instead of a prime concern with how people will have to use the building, Breuer reduces architectural considerations to the delicate question of how a tower will relate visually to the terminal building below it. Meanwhile, *Architectural Forum,* a professional magazine, applauded the design, "The deep cantilever-recess under the slab of the tower will divorce the latter from the Beaux-Arts palace below it; and the studied restraint and neutrality of the new tower's exteriors will further set these back visually from the ornate façades of the present terminal. . . ."[3]

The reaction of one of the leading professional journals to the environmental blight Breuer was helping to create is typical of reform rationalization. Accusing the system, they pat the professional on the back for making the best of a bad

situation. "It would be silly to blame Breuer (or any other architect) for the kind of unrestricted land speculation that makes such buildings inevitable," says *Architectural Forum*. Better that a "good" architect like Breuer got the commission than a "bad" one. The magazine ends with the moral, "as professionals, it seems that architects should try to make the best of the world *as it is*—before somebody else fouls it up even further."[4] With this dreary and negative conclusion, the magazine sums up the profession, unself-consciously and without irony. But is the professional really a tool of whatever system he operates in? Does he have a responsibility for his acts other than to do his job better than someone else? Is the engineer who designed a more painless gas chamber to be lauded as a "realist," or the scientist who designs a cleaner nuclear bomb a more responsible professional? Even Adolf Eichmann congratulated himself that his efficient operations made his victims' pain easier to bear.* Every individual ought to be responsible for his own acts, and participating in an immoral act is simply immoral. To use the argument that you prevent a person less sensitive to the problem from engaging in the same act hardly exonerates the person whose direct participation after all makes it possible for the act to occur.

The example of Breuer's proposed work at Grand Central is just an up-to-date example of the architect's traditional role in this country. The kind of cultural trappings, devoid of humane social content, that Breuer was providing for that environmental disaster has been in vogue at least since the beginning of the city-planning movement.

* Eichmann claimed more than once that his organizational gifts, the coordination of evacuations and deportations achieved by his officials, had in fact helped his victims; it had made their fate easier. "If this thing had to be done at all, it was better that it be done in good order." (Arendt, Hannah, *Eichmann in Jerusalem*, Viking Press, New York [paperback], 1964, p. 190.)

THE FACTORY CAMP

I can't make strong enough tribute to this city [New York]. I was born here. Ninety-nine per cent of the things that have happened to me came about because of it. I can't mourn the disappearance of a lot of old buildings. The city's beauty, such as it is, is increasing, not lessening. I seem to hear less noise; it strikes me the town is cleaner. So we lost some fairly attractive apartment buildings on Park Avenue. What have we got instead? A Seagram Building, a Union Carbide Building, a Lever House, a great Renaissance. We're off again; we're moving; we're alive, dynamic, virile.

> —Jerome Brody, president of Restaurant Associates, owner of the Four Seasons, the Forum of the Twelve Caesars, Rikers and other restaurants[5]

New York City is always there. If you've been there a while and gone away and come back it hasn't moved an inch. Not since Henry Hudson shit on the Indians. Then Peter Stuyvesant shit on Henry Hudson who was shit on by Nelson Rockefeller who was shit on by King Kong or Consolidated Edison. New York City is the largest pay toilet on earth and a lot of pretty people have learned to crawl under the door.

> —Hugh Romney, member of the Hog Farm Commune[6]

While the idea of designing all parts of a city at one time can be traced to grid layouts of Roman military camps, to medieval star-shaped geometrics (again with military implications) and to early colonial examples such as Philadelphia and Savannah, the real impetus for rationalizing the form and development of large American cities came from the expansion of industrial capitalism in the 1900s. This phenomenon was to make the nineteenth-century city a giant factory camp, needing space for its machines, techniques for bringing raw material to the machines, sending out finished products, means for producing energy to feed machines, vast quantities of storage space for the workers, and office and government buildings to administer the workers' lives. The magnitude and complexity of this agglomeration meant there were few decisions individuals could make in a city or town that would not affect others. The effects of the factory camp became especially apparent in the use of land. In order to locate industry next to residences, lots were subdivided into sizes that led to congestion, and buildings for the poor were quickly thrown together. The stampede for wealth that the Industrial Revolution promoted with the factory camp as one of its products led to environments of physical disaster and social chaos.

The Chicago World's Fair in 1893 is often cited as the jumping-off point for the city-planning movement. This "White City," which got its name from the plaster-finished buildings, was the model architects could point to as an

answer to the dirty slums of the factory camp city. With the exception of Louis Sullivan's Transportation Building, it was distinguished as one of the most pompous collections of copied Classic and Renaissance architecture ever built. Lest its more enduring value to city planning be misstated, it was the first time in modern American history that so large a collection of big buildings had been designed on a consistent architectural theme at one time—a dubious notion under which many of our present city design concepts still labor. Architectural consistency is not necessarily beautiful, desirable or an appropriate model for the complex activities of urban life. Nor is "consistency" an appropriate way to relate architecture to a democratic political process; a democratic architecture would search for forms that could evolve from a complexity of design interests rather than submerge them into "unified," "consistent" themes. Daniel Burnham, the architect charged with coordinating the fair's design, went on to make a pronouncement oft-quoted by architects

139

Chicago World's Fair, 1893

which equaled the pomposity of the fair's architecture. "Make no little plans," he said; "they have no magic to stir men's blood." That fair was a landmark for many urban designers; no longer would they limit themselves to only a building or small part of the city. Instead, concepts would be developed to bring "order" to the entire city. Burnham himself prepared "big" plans for San Francisco, Chicago and Manila. While only parts of these plans ever got built, their effect on city designers was a lasting one.

In Burnham's plans, the concept of a "hierarchy" of uses was elaborated. This hierarchy begins with the idea of the "big plan" or "strong statement." It also involves breaking the city into a number of "land use" categories, like "housing," "commercial," "industrial," "institutional." The institutional buildings, like city halls and government buildings, are usually at the top of the hierarchy, since they're considered "important" buildings. "Housing" and "commercial" buildings are somewhere in the middle, with housing often used as background or infill for the design. "Industrial" is at the bottom of the hierarchy, since it's usually considered the most obnoxious land use.

140

Burnham's own description of the hierarchy in the Manila plan could also describe his and other planners' approach to later plans for other American cities.

Among building groups the first in importance, the Government or National Group—which would include Capital Building and department Buildings, is located on the present Camp Wallace. . . . Grouping itself closely about the Capital Building at the center it forms a hollow square opening out westward toward the sea. The gain in dignity by grouping these buildings in a single formal mass has dictated this arrangement, the beauty and convenience of which has been put to the test in notable examples from the days of Old Rome to the Louvre and Versailles of modern times.

The eastern front of the capital group faces a semi-circular plaza from whose center radiates a street system communicating with all section of the city—an arrangement entirely fitting for both practical and sentimental reasons; practical because the center of governmental activity should be readily accessible from all sides; sentimental because *every section of the Capital City should look with deference toward the symbol of the Nation's power*. . . .

The Court House or Hall of Justice is given a separate location south of the main group and heading the vista down the avenue which passes the east front of the Capital. . . . The Hall of Justice . . . represents sentimentally and practically the highest function of civilized society. Upon the authority of law depends the lives and property of all citizens; and the buildings which constitute the visible expression of law, its symbol of dignity and power, should be given the utmost beauty in their location, arrangement, architectural treatment and approaches. . . .[7] (author's italics)

The Manila plan was to be the appropriate architectural dressing for the spoils of America's imperialistic ventures following the Spanish-American War. Burnham's commission came after the United States, having defeated "imperialist" Spain, brutally suppressed the popular independence movement led by Emilio Aguinaldo and took over the Philippines as a possession. Burnham's work along with that of United States Consulting Architect in the Philippines, William E. Parsons, would provide, according to *Architectural Record,* the proper artistic model for the "uncultured" captive population to imitate.

> Some time in the future, when the Filipino finally settles down to the development of things artistic, we may look for the creation of an indigenous architecture expressive of the country and its people. Until then very little can reasonably be expected from a race without deep artistic tradition or scientific knowledge. In the meantime, the buildings erected and the city plan improvements executed by our Government will stand as worthy examples, setting a high standard from which in the coming years native architects can derive abundant inspiration.[8]

Burnham's development of large-scale planning was based largely on the neo-Baroque model which Baron Haussmann, one of history's earliest urban renewers, had used for Paris in the nineteenth century. Haussmann's star-shaped street layouts were supposed to give a visual order and artistic organization to an entire city—what some Parisians called "strategic beautification."* He could tear through the congested streets of Paris with his boulevards radiating from monumental city squares since he had the power of an autocratic regime behind him—a regime, moreover, which feared the narrow streets where soldiers could be attacked by the street mobs. Today, techniques like armored cars, tear gas and Mace provide more effective, though less aesthetic, ways of controlling people in the cities.

The essence of hierarchical architecture is to visually

---

* Haussman called himself an "artist in demolition." His plans which consisted of replacing the narrow, winding streets of Paris with wide monumental boulevards were seen as ways of preventing erection of barricades by the Parisian working class. (Benjamin, Walter, "Paris, Capital of the 19th Century," in *New Left Review*, No. 48, March–April 1968, p. 86.)

142

reinforce hierarchical political structures. The more magnificent and monumental the official public places, the more trivial becomes the citizen's personal environment and the more he tends to be awed by the official environment. This was the essence of Burnham's proposal that "every section of the Capital City should look with deference towards the symbol of the nation's power. . . ." It's an old game, historically played not only by the governments but by churches and other institutions. It forms the basis for present-day visions of glorifying government through architectural propaganda.

METAPHORS OF FASCISM

In 1969 Daniel P. Moynihan, President Nixon's chief planner in residence, addressed the Joint American Institute of Architects and the Royal Architecture Institute of Canada convention. Bemoaning the loss of public-building symbols, he said:

> . . . the American polity—the experience as well as the

Richard Nixon with advisor Daniel P. Moynihan (at right)

sense of community and shared conviction—has been impaired, has atrophied in our time because of the retreat from architecture and public buildings as a conscious element of public policy and a purposeful instrument for the expression of public purpose.[9]

According to Moynihan, the inability of political leaders to insist on right kinds of architecture has led to:

. . . a steady deterioration in the quality of public buildings and spaces, and with it a decline in the symbols of public unity and common purpose with which the citizen can identify, of which he can be proud, and by which he can know what he shares with his fellow citizens.[10]

Some years earlier, another person in another country

Architecture of the Third Reich, Munich

Proposed architecture for U.S. government buildings, Washington, D.C.

who was also to become a public figure wrote about a similar concern:

> . . . our cities of the present lack the outstanding symbol of national community which, we must therefore not be surprised to find, sees no symbol of itself in the cities. The inevitable result is a desolation whose practical effect is the total indifference of the big-city dweller to the destiny of his city.[11]

That was Adolf Hitler describing his views on city design in *Mein Kampf*. For government leaders, struck with a vision of the historic purpose of architectural propaganda, a major theme of building design is symbolic monuments to commemorate the present glory to future generations. According to Moynihan:

> The task of this less than all-powerful nation is to show to the world and to ourselves that, sensing our limitations, we know also our strengths. The surest sign of whether we have done this will reside in the buildings and public places which we shall build in our time, and for which we will be remembered or forgotten in history.[12]

145

According to Hitler:

> Every great period finds the final expression of its values in its buildings. . . .[13]
>
> Such visible demonstration of the higher qualities of a people will, as the experience of history proves, remain for thousands of years as an unquestionable testimony not only to the greatness of a people, but also to their moral right to exist.[14]

In the early 1960s Moynihan was actually given the opportunity to affect the design of federal government buildings. He drafted the "Guiding Principles on Federal Architecture," which President Kennedy announced in 1962.

According to these principles:

> The policy shall be to provide requisite and adequate facilities in an architectural style and form which is distinguished and which will reflect the dignity, enterprise, vigor, and stability of the American National Government.[15]

Architecture of American government buildings, Washington, D.C.

Architecture of the Third Reich, Berlin

Again, Hitler had a similar vision of government vitality and symbols. Describing the German Congress Building, he said:

> . . . the spirit of our times is embodied here . . . in this eternal monument to German rebirth, in this stone symbol of German greatness, German vitality, and German culture.[16]

The models Hitler used to justify the need for public symbols included ancient temples, stadia, medieval town halls and cathedrals which had dominated the city. This, of

147

course, would be the essence of fascist architecture—glorifying the state by making individual efforts seem insignificant. Said Hitler:

> For what the ancient had before his eyes was less the humble houses of private owners than the magnificent edifices of the whole community. Compared to them the dwelling house really sank to an insignificant object of secondary importance.[17]

Unfortunately for those in the residential buildings, this model of people homes as of "secondary importance" is essentially the same one that some designers still use to glorify not only the state but other "special" institutions of our society. Discussing his design for an urban-renewal project in Boston, for example, Araldo Cossutta, partner in the I. M. Pei architectural firm, stated, "Buildings engage in a dialogue like actors on a stage among themselves and with us as spectators. Some buildings must be stars and others only chorus, some must shine and some must support."[18]

The star in this case will be a church building, while the "only chorus" are to be several continuous-façade apartment buildings forming an anonymous backdrop to the church. The hierarchical intent is clear: The church is the dominant higher use while the living quarters which "only" house people are secondary.

Writing for the American Institute of Architects, Paul D. Spreiregen described a similar theory for architects to use in designing entire metropolitan areas:

> A metropolitan design structure is essential to every architect working at the scale of a building group or a single building. Since it reveals the situation of his building functionally and visually, it furnishes important clues to the ways each building is approached, seen, and used. *It gives the city an essential skeleton within which special buildings and clusters are the vital organs and in which the lesser buildings are the flesh. A design structure is the*

148

framework for foreground and background architecture working together.[19] (author's italics)

The metaphoric aesthetic language of "stars" and "choruses," "organs" and "flesh," is a revealing example of how architects have traditionally removed their concern from the essential nature of building design, which should be to provide habitable places for people to live. The point is not that these architects see themselves promoting fascist or repressive environments; it is that in fact they do promote such places. And the way they can obscure this fact from themselves and others is to present their work in the absence of an explicit political analysis. In Hitler's description, he at least used a language which made it clear that the requirements of a fascist architecture were to make the person's dwelling "an insignificant object of secondary importance." In this country the aesthetic metaphors of the architects' language instead obscures the real nature of many of their designs, not only to their clients and the larger population, but to themselves as well.

In this language, buildings are described metaphorically as physical *objects* in relation to each other rather than as containers for human activity. Architects often criticize each other's buildings by describing whether one building appears to be visually good or bad when seen next to another. The people who use the buildings are presumably also "spectators" to this phenomenon and pass similar judgments on what is happening—that tall "tower" type "foreground" building looks good or bad in relation to a low "slab" type "background" building. "Buildings engage in dialogue," said Cossutta, "like actors on a stage *among themselves* and *with us as spectators*."

The usefulness of this metaphoric language to those who rule lies in its acceptance as the language of *aesthetic* ideology rather than the language of *political* ideology. The architects' language doesn't deal in phrases like "the glorification of a fascist state" or "the exploitation of workers."

149

Rather it describes phenomena in the poetic terms which can be appreciated and criticized on ostensibly non-political grounds by the cultured middle class. In doing so, it obscures the political implications of the projects it describes from this bourgeois class and other architects. It encourages debate over the aesthetic appropriateness of a particular architectural project rather than questions about the political consequences.

The "Architects' Plan for Boston," prepared by an American Institute of Architects committee in 1961, is a good case of how architects provide an aesthetic mask for politically repressive acts. Their plan, recommending construction of an "Inner Belt" expressway around downtown Boston, followed an older proposal by the state highway department. The AIA committee made no mention of political or social effect on the 10,000 people, most of them poor, who would be displaced by the action. The architects chose instead to talk in more soothing cultural terms—"the coming renaissance of the cities," the problems of "visual composition," "scale," "transition" and "the timeless pace of man." "[In] the coming renaissance of our cities," said the AIA committee, "many questions of visual composition and detail will cry out for an expert: the architect is suited by talent and training for the job." "To provide a scale large enough to be understood at sixty miles an hour, to design for the timeless pace of the man on foot and to make the transition between them is our essential problem." In their more detailed suggestions for designing the highway, social value judgments are masked by aesthetic language. According to the committee, "If an industrial area must be bisected, the roadway should be elevated to preserve visual continuity."[20]

What these planners as artists are saying here is that the person who happens to work in a factory or near a factory will have to put up with the noise, fumes and lack of sunlight that are associated with elevated road structures in order "to preserve visual continuity." The aesthetic concept

150

of "visual continuity" (which presumably means if you are standing on one side of a road you can see across to the other side) is used to rationalize a blighted environment for factory workers, a rationalization the planners can maintain since they and their clients don't work in factories.

Some "theories of urban form" are hardly even this circumspect in disguising the interests they're promoting. An American Institute of Architects–sponsored book on *Urban Design* suggests the design of roads and highways be treated as a way of shielding the sensibilities of those of us driving to and from downtown from the "depressing" views we are forced to pass through during our daily automobile trips.

According to this book:

> The gray areas are not quite slums—they are the service quarters of the city, the place where small businesses may begin and, often, where major ones thrive. They are not glamorous areas, but they may be very much alive, if not with color then at least with people living and working. The gray areas of the city are a necessity.
>
> For urban design, this fact of urban life should not come as a disappointment but as a realization to be reckoned with. What can urban design do for the gray areas?[21]

Written under the guidance of some of the most distinguished "urban designers" in the country,* the book explains what urban design can do for the gray areas:

> Perhaps the real defect of the gray zone is that *we* see too much of it. *We* pass by large extents of it on *our* new elevated auto expressways as *we* soar above the streets

* According to the Acknowledgments written by William H. Scheick, "The articles were written and illustrated by Paul D. Spreiregen under the guidance of the American Institute of Architects Urban Design Committee's members and others. The Committee Members were: Edmund N. Bacon, Frederich Bigger, FAIA, Charles A. Blessing, FAIA, Kenneth Brooks, Henry Churchill, FAIA (deceased), Vernon Demars, FAIA, Carl Feiss, FAIA, Robert L. Geddes, George N. Hall, Donald H. Lutes, Albert Mayer, FAIA, Matthew L. Rockwell, Archibald C. Rogers, Nicholas Satterlee, Clarence Stein, FAIA, Harry Weese, FAIA, Arch R. Winter, Gordon G. Wittenberg.

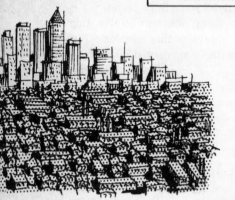

Gray areas are vital functional
and physical adjuncts to the
center of the city.

We can diminish their visual
effects by shielding our approach views. At the same time
we can relieve the gray areas
with open spaces.

toward the center city. *We* pass through much of it as
we proceed along our center city's major arteries. *We* see it
as *we* approach the center in the morning on the way to
work and in the evening on our way home. Its too frequent
sight taxes *our* patience. *The answer may lie in application*
of theatrics to the urban scene. If the gray area is too frequently visible, too depressing because it is too much in

152

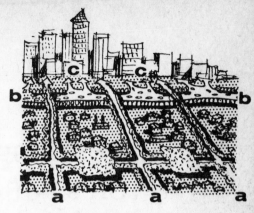

Better still, we can link them to the center with their own system of paths (a), our expressways can bypass the gray areas (b), and both systems can enter the central city together (c).

our presence, perhaps *we* can arrange *our* major routes to avoid it, to bypass it, to give *us* views of the parts of the city *we* hold in higher esteem. In the Renaissance, architects were able to recast the service elements of buildings into what appeared to be blank walls which could form entrance courts or the walls bordering a long passage. Could *we* not do this on the larger scale of the city? Could *we* not conceal, or at least play down, that which distorts the image of *our* central city's better self?[22] (author's italics)

Of course, some people (guess who?) must live and work in the "depressing" gray areas. Our (guess who?) problem is to build our expressways and walls, plant our trees and shrubs in a way that will keep us safe from the blight.

The more architecture can be described in the morally neutral currency of "aesthetics," devoid of political content for the people affected, the more elite and the more removed from the political review of ordinary people become the experts who use this currency. Meanwhile, as those who practice architecture, criticize architecture, those who teach architecture and those who learn about and "appreciate" architecture continue to see it in "aesthetic" rather than political terms, the more useful this "aesthetic" becomes to those who rule. For the rulers are no longer repressing people with their highways and urban-renewal projects; they are supposedly bringing them progress and culture.

153

V

Excess Baggage: Professionalism and Alienation

If I were trying to run things my way, I would do everything that I could to teach everybody that they were not able to run things like me. I would teach that to build something else meant that whoever wanted to do it would have to become like me. I would finally teach that I was the only person who knew enough to make other people like me. If I could manage all that, I wouldn't have to let people know they were slaves.

—Charlie Cobb, SNCC Field Secretary[1]

A scientific body entrusted with the government of society would soon end by devoting itself not to science but to quite another interest. And that, as is the case with all established powers, would consist in its endeavor to perpetuate itself in power and consolidating its position by rendering the society placed in its care even more stupid and consequently ever more in need of being governed and directed by such a body.

—Mikhail Bakunin, anarchist philosopher[2]

"THE PRACTICE of asking what the community wants," said architect Hugh Hardy, discussing a building he designed in a black ghetto, "is not really helpful to the architect—except politically, or to clarify the program. The community can only think of what it knows. It can't help the architect in his

154

architectural problem."[3] This attitude which forgets to ask the basic question of *why* people's ideas about environment are so limited goes on to reinforce the expert's confidence in himself. Since the people's ideas are narrow, according to this argument, they need more of what the professional has to offer; rationalizing the status quo, *because of* the status quo, simply serves to maintain the status quo.

One obvious answer to the why is that when you live in a society with few incentives to develop skills for designing your own environment, you simply don't develop these skills. Seeing this lack of skills, this "inadequacy," our own self-image as professionals is reinforced and the cycle is perpetuated. By debating among ourselves, studying among ourselves and rewarding ourselves, we have come to have less and less tolerance for what we define as non-expert opinions. In giving each other prizes for each other's buildings, we don't bother to ask the occupants of the buildings being considered. The magazine *Progressive Architecture,* for example, gives its annual awards specifically to projects that haven't been built yet. Only recently has the American Institute of Architects required that one of the jurors for its annual competition actually visit buildings they are considering for awards. One day they may even require one of the jurors be someone who uses the building.

By playing the game this way, we have as professionals helped make it especially hard for people to develop places suited to the way they might choose to live; what design skills they might have developed have remained dormant. Meanwhile, with "culture" relegated to the experts, the mass of the population is left to sublimate their design potential through magazines, "art appreciation" courses and real-estate advertisements. So, in addition to the bureaucratic maze of paper and time people must follow to create a suitable environment for themselves, they must also adapt their needs to professionals who have trained themselves to pass judgment on what other people's environments should be like.

The professional societies take special care to communicate the environmental expert's importance and to bemoan the blight and chaos which follow when he isn't used. One of the guidelines set down for its members by the American Institute of Architects (AIA) is that they participate actively in the life of their community in order "to project the image of professional competence which is basic to a popular confidence in architects."[4] One way to strengthen this image, says the AIA, is to do volunteer work in poor neighborhoods. After planning work for the poor became popular, especially among the more socially motivated students, it became safe for the AIA to recommend its use in image-

What did the jurors say behind closed doors?
How did the jurors come to their decisions?
What did they say about the entries, new planning
directions, controversial designs?
Which socio/economic events did they feel should
be reflected in today's architecture?

PROGRESSIVE ARCHITECTURE'S

17th ANNUAL DESIGN AWARDS ISSUE

plus 11 other exciting P/A issues

YOURS NOW FOR HALF PRICE!

building. "Nothing can more plainly show the community
the profession's interest in its life and future," said the
AIA's public-relations guide, "than this type of voluntary
participation."[5] Offering still other ways to project the profession's image, the AIA says:

An effective promotion can be mounted by persuading the
mayor or city council to issue a proclamation naming a
given week in the year as "Community Design Week."
This is better than having an "Architects' Week," which

appears self-interested and immediately narrows the scope of public interest.[6]

Questions about right and wrong professional practice are to be decided within the special society of the profession—not by outsiders. William H. Scheick, executive director of the AIA, complained about the "baiting" his organization was getting from outsiders. Without bothering to specify what the criticism was, he said:

Thanks to vigorous growth, progressive policies and productive action, we are too busy to be bothered. Our best critics are within the family, always figuring out how to do better while enduring our growing pains.[7]

Roy D. Murphy, president of the Society of American Registered Architects (ARA), AIA's competitor professional organization, took a slightly less tolerant position toward criticism:

Those who don't even recognize what has already happened in this profession, and resist and criticize the changes are hardly worth being concerned about.[8]

As professionals come to perceive themselves as the keepers of a cultural monopoly, they come to feel a unique sense of power in shaping other people's environments. Speaking of the need to "return the architect to the position of leadership in the new building industry," Mr. Murphy presents the view of the architect controlling the design of all buildings.

We are proponents of the architect as an artist, sensitive to the needs of emotional satisfaction as a part of the building process. However, we are determined first to develop organization and systems that will allow design creativity to become effective. We want the architectural touch applied to ALL buildings, rather than just the limited 20% that are controlled by architects at this time.[9]

And with the same immodest approach, the AIA's president proposed a similar role for the architect. According to

Mr. Scheick, beginning in 1958, the AIA's "vision expanded to encompass the entire creative process for building mankind's physical environment." Which sounds as though there isn't much room for many people outside the "family"; he is actually more humble. "Whoever is concerned with solving the socio-economic-political problems is our ally," said Scheick. "What is good for humanity is good for our allies and good for us." That may seem as if just about everybody in favor of virtue and motherhood could get in on the act. But the AIA's executive director takes special care to single out the important ones: "We are not alone in our desire to work for a better environment. The other *professions* and many *powerful segments of the building industry* share this desire."[10] (author's italics) Thus, once again, an alliance of the "powerful segments of industry" and the experts will find answers to our "socio-economic-political problems." Those of us who are presumably to be the beneficiaries of this largesse would do well to ponder the already accumulated result of this alliance in solving the problems of education, job training, housing, and transportation.

AN ARCHITECTURE FOR ARCHITECTS

The Street has always been an interesting symbol in middle class American life. It was always the place to avoid. There is "violence in the Streets," "bad people in the Streets," and "danger in the Streets." It was always "let's keep the kids off the Streets," as honkie America moved from inside to inside. It is in the Streets that we will make our struggle. The Streets belong to the people! Long live the Flower-Cong of the gutters!

—Abbie Hoffman[11]

[Park Avenue] formed one of the few convincingly imperial avenues of the world. . . . seen against the incoherent masses westward or against the older solid buildings to the north, Lever's was an elegant, pristine object, and might have been considered a special adornment to the Avenue, the breaking of whose continuity might thus have been condoned. But when the building to the north of it was reclad in a glass and plastic skin, imitating Lever's, it became apparent that Lever's itself owed everything to the pre-existing civility of the street.

—Vincent Scully, architectural critic[12]

With architects' rewards determined by whether or not their work appears in visual media such as books, magazines and museums, there is a stronger incentive for them to focus on visual aspects of building design than, for example, to consider how comfortable the buildings are for the people who use them. Not having to live in the places they produce gives architects a further opportunity to do this, since they don't have to justify their design in terms of their own living patterns. Strangely enough many modern architects I know choose to live in remodeled old homes rather than modern buildings. They will admit it's the "warmth" and "comfortable feeling" of the old building as opposed to the rigid geometry of modern architecture that attracts them.

The once-removed quality of the architects from their clients and the visual nature of the professional reward system have induced architects to develop a theory of design for their clients concerned with the way a building ought to be seen; architecture becomes a "look at" experience rather than a "live in" one. The result is to remove further the process of architecture from the ken of ordinary mortals who must live in the architects' buildings. By focusing on the visual aspects of building design as a cultural phenomenon to be understood by people who visit art museums or read architecture books, architects proceed to deal with architecture in aesthetic terms rather than in terms of human use. It is uncouth to speak about how a building "feels"—one must rationalize the enjoyment of a building in terms of its mass, its proportions, its composition, the clarity of the plan, its significance for our time, much as you would a painting. A further shift of architectural practice from considerations of humane use has come from the almost religious attitude that has developed about the ways of "honestly" showing the techniques used in constructing a building. According to a tenet of such gospel, the observer must view a building as it behaves according to structural principles. One approach to this kind of aesthetics comes from Louis I. Kahn, a well-known architect and theorist. "I would think that if you are dealing with a column," said Kahn, "you must give it a beam. You cannot have a column without a beam. It is an elemental thing. You can't have a column and a slab; you know the slab has a beam inside of it."[13] Another rule holds that the appearance of building details must be as honest as possible. When two different materials are joined to each other, for example, the joining point must clearly show the two materials as separate from each other, so as not to be ambiguous to the observer. Miës van der Rohe, the revered, German-born patriarch of American architects and a master of this approach, once claimed, "God is in the details."

This sort of mind-bending stricture was stuffed into me and other architecture students almost ten years ago. A reading of the architectural journals, or sitting in at review sessions in a number of the major architectural schools today, will demonstrate that it still holds sway. It was only after I left school and began to work with people who had little to do with "architecture" that I realized how far removed the profession had become from real needs. Perceptual qualities of honesty was a game invented and played by those who spend hours at a drafting board thinking about what would be nice to *look at*. For people who actually *use* an environment, needs grow out of much more tangible and sometimes seemingly mundane aspects of how environments are used, not their visual appearance as a justification for an aesthetic theory. People are concerned about supervising

161

children at play, peeing in the hallways, making locks that can't be broken, having large enough kitchens to entertain friends (the kitchen is not just a place to prepare food), and the problem of adults being able to get away from children and children being able to get away from adults.

In architectural school, "community" was good because it allowed you to put a lot of buildings together in ways that would visually "define" interesting spaces; our models for this were the medieval hill towns of Italy. But in the ghettos, many families were trying to get away from a sense of forced community—a community where people were packed together with other families because our economic system gave them no other choices.

In architectural school, we were told that the most important thing to do was make a "strong statement." We were to be the "master builders," setting the pattern of new visual conditions for people to perceive. The important thing was the single, overriding "concept" to which many things could adapt. We would design a shopping center and the instructor would say "put it all under one roof"—that was a strong statement—find a shape in which all things could fit. Always the single idea, the gimmick which would capture your client's imagination. All this, of course, went back to Daniel Burnham's dictum for inspiring the client. "Make no small plans," Burnham had said; "they have no magic to stir men's blood." We were being trained to be super salesmen of our products and if the needs didn't exist we would invent them—much as manufacturers do with their products through advertising. Simple, direct, bold statements would sell ideas.

An architect told me how he got a planning board that seemed to know little about design to accept his plan for rehousing people from a squatter slum. The design, which could be described as a simple diagram, he explained, made it easy for the board to understand. The people could adapt their needs to the design in a variety of ways, putting up

162

walls here, leaving some out there. By considering individual needs, such adaptations, of course, begin to make sense; but they are, after all, *adaptations*. The individual must adapt to the over-all design, instead of the other way around. Meanwhile, the over-all design grows from the need of one professional, who doesn't live in the environment, to explain his design in simplistic terms, to groups of bureaucrats who also don't live in the environment (but control it through access to public funds). The need to *explain* the design thus becomes a prime motivation for what the design finally turns out to be.

I recall another case of working on a project where several teams of architects had prepared designs for different sections of Harlem. At one of our reviews a team displayed a design with a huge open-air plaza at one end of the community. Each side of the plaza was about a quarter of a mile long. In a northern city, outdoor plazas have limited use during the year and in the winter they are pretty miserable to walk through. I asked one of the team why they had the plaza and why it was so large. Pointing to the bottom of a large map on the wall behind him, he explained the design needed something large to give "balance" to the lower left—that was the reason! Seated in the room were a number of architects and architectural historians from some of the best-known architectural schools in the country. No one even laughed.

As the "urban crisis" has taken shape and architects became city planners and urban designers, their "statements" have unfortunately become places where vast numbers of people live. Buildings as sculptural objects set in large open spaces with grass and trees have become a favorite urban composition for planners who saw the city as their canvas. The idea was first promoted by Le Corbusier, the Swiss-French architect who saw the setting of large buildings in park areas as an answer to the congestion of the cities. You could get as many people in the city this way, argued Le

Corbusier, but by putting them in tall, densely packed buildings, the remaining ground below could be used for healthy play, walking and taking in the sun. Instead of being just another façade in the city, the building in this conception would become a sculptural object, properly displayed by the open space around it. Excepting the obvious advantages of providing more sunlight, this idea has little to do with a useful environment. The large public-housing and redevelopment projects, typical examples of the concept in action, act as barriers between neighborhoods and the large open spaces tend to isolate people from one another. Tall "tower" and "slab" buildings, as the professionals like to call them, make it especially hard for parents to watch over younger children.

But the buildings in the park, the strong statements, the approach to building as simple forms, are only the more traditional of the planners' architectural theories. A peek at what some of the most "avant-garde" professionals are doing is even more frightening.

THE ARCHITECTURE OF COUNTER-REVOLUTION

Robert Venturi is considered by many architects to be one of the most important and influential architects and theorists today. In his introduction to Venturi's book *Complexity and Contradiction in Architecture*, Vincent Scully, one of this country's better-known architectural critics, called it "probably the most important writing on the making of architecture since Le Corbusier's *Vers une Architecture* of 1923." "The future," he said, "will value it among the few basic texts of our time." Another critic proclaimed:

For to a whole school of young architects and students this book may be adopted as a battle-cry of a new movement—another banner to be unfurled by the longhaired, restless, inquiring, selfconscious NOW generation, who seek in every way to smash the past five to ten (or more) years.[14]

164

And another followed:

> At last an architect who has the courage to write about
> architecture! . . . Venturi's observations ought to be car-
> ried further as soon as possible.[15]

In this book, Venturi, whose own buildings he describes as
"pop architecture," begins with a point Paul Rudolph and
other architects have made: that modern architects have
traditionally looked for simple solutions to complex building
programs in order to achieve a simplified building form. He
argues that in exploiting the complexity of needs that building must serve, a more vital architecture could be produced.
Quoting Rudolph, he notes:

> . . . it is characteristic of the twentieth century that
> architects are highly selective in determining which prob-
> lems they want to solve. Mies [van der Rohe], for in-
> stance, makes wonderful buildings only because he ignores
> many aspects of a building. If he solved more problems,
> his buildings would be far less potent.[16]

The architect, says Venturi,

> . . . can exclude important considerations only at the risk
> of separating architecture from the experience of life and
> the needs of society. If some problems prove insoluble,
> he can express this: in an inclusive rather than exclusive
> kind of architecture there is room for the fragment, for
> contradiction, for improvisation, and for the tension these
> produce.[17]

This had the appealing ring of a direct, anarchist approach to architecture, free of the constraints of the usual
formal design theories bent on a rigid categorizing of form.
He seemed to be saying that architecture could be ambiguous, contradictory, but growing from "the experience of
life." He was arguing against the simplistic view of Le
Corbusier, whose call for "great primary forms" which were
"distinct . . . and without ambiguity" no doubt led to Le
Corbusier's city-planning techniques, using simple tower
buildings in parklike settings.[18]

But in reality, Venturi seems to have little concern with "the experience of life." I searched the entire book for any description of how people use architecture; there was hardly a word about it—instead the same aesthetic jargon. A series of building plans, elevations and photos show how certain architectural qualities make a building seem more complex and contradictory. There is almost no analysis of whether the buildings used as examples really accommodate the complexity and contradiction of human activities they were intended to serve. The important thing is simply the appearance of architectural forms. Typical is Venturi's analysis of Le Corbusier's Millowner's Building in Ahmedabad, India:

From the important approach from the south, the repetitive pattern of the brise-soleil invokes rhythms which are violently broken by the entrance void, the ramp, and the stairs. These latter elements, consisting of varying diagonals, create violent superadjacencies from the front, in relation to the rectangular static floor divisions within the boxlike form. The juxtapositions of diagonals and perpendiculars also create contradictory directions: the meeting of the ramp and stairs is only slightly softened by the exceptionally large void and by the modified rhythm of the elements at that part of the facade.[19]

What Venturi was doing was simply trying to replace existing "look-at" architectural theories with one of his own. This time it's a look-at theory calling for complexity and contradiction instead of simple forms. He calls for buildings which *appear* to answer complex problems but whose complexity is derived by creating aesthetic rules about what makes one building visually *seem* to be more complex and contradictory than another. In this "most important writing on the making of architecture" since 1923, the author can claim to talk directly about architecture without even considering its social use. That's not my analysis, it's Venturi's. "I make no special attempt to relate architecture to other things," he says. "I have not tried to 'improve the connec-

166

tions between science and technology on the one hand, and the humanities and the social sciences on the other . . . and make of architecture a more human social art.' I try to talk about architecture rather than around it."[20]

By divorcing an environment from the people who use it, and by focusing simply on visual characteristics of his own choosing, he can make the elevated trains which have blighted the poor areas of many American cities appear to be an important element to be used in the urban designer's palette.

The nineteenth century American "elevated" which was juxtaposed above the street anticipated the multi-level city like Sigmond's 1958 plan for Berlin which proposed a multi-level city with large-scale circulation elevated above the local traffic. In this kind of superimposition the degree of separation lies between the changing, almost incidental superimpositions of forms that are very separate in space and the interpenetration of superimpositions on the same plane. Superadjacencies at this intermediate degree are closely related but not touching, like the configuration of a separated lining.[21]

He can call the Buon Pastore (an orphanage near Rome) "admittedly questionable as an asylum for little girls," yet go on to talk about how it

. . . astonishingly composes a multitude of diverse parts into a difficult whole. At all levels of scale it is an example of inflections successively directed toward different centers —toward the short facade in the front, or the anticlimactically small dome near the center of the complex, with its unusually big cupola. When you stand close enough to see a smaller element of inflection, you sometimes need to turn almost 180 degrees to see its counterpart at a great distance. An element of suspense is introduced when you move around the enormous building. You are aware of elements related by inflection to elements already seen or not yet seen, like the unraveling of a symphony. As a fragment in plan and elevation, the asymmetrical composition of each wing is wrought with tensions and implications concerning the symmetrical whole.[22]

Yet in spite of his disclaimer against making "architecture a more social art," Venturi attempts to do just that—to make an explicit relationship between social values and the form of his buildings. He begins with an accurate analysis of some of the most disturbing social conditions of our society.

Industry promotes expensive industrial and electronic research but not architectural experiments, and the Federal government diverts subsidies toward air transportation, communication, and the vast enterprises of war or, as they call it, national security, rather than towards the forces for the direct enhancement of life.[23]

But Venturi's architectural solution to this dilemma is incredible. He says they should

. . . accept their modest role rather than disguise it. . . . The architect who would *accept his role as combiner of significant old cliches—valid banalties*—in new contexts as his condition within a society that directs its best efforts, its big money, and its elegant technologies elsewhere, *can ironically express in this indirect way a true concern for society's inverted scale of values.*[24] (author's italics)

Architecture as social comment? Architecture as satire? Venturi's approach is like the white man's patronizing approval of the plantation darky's humor which expresses his passivity and self-abasement. Venturi's "ironic convention," or "dualities" or "superadjacencies" and the like, are collective flights into impotence surrounded by a banjo-accompanied fantasy of ever more vulgar design. There just happen to be people living in those "ironically expressed" buildings. By Venturi's standards, wouldn't the designers of public housing and urban renewal be among the great social

168

critics of our time—or aren't their designs ironic enough? Or how about a special award to Marcel Breuer for his proposed pile of office building on top of Grand Central Terminal? Think of that contradiction between the Beaux Arts terminal and the modern office mass. But what about all those workers who would have to live in that mess? Is the contradiction and irony really enough to sustain them? I tend to doubt that the so-called "longhaired, restless, inquiring, self-conscious NOW generation" is going to buy the program.

If Venturi had any social values in mind when he wrote this book, he left little doubt, a few years later, that they were hardly his prime concern. In an article written with Denise Scott Brown, Venturi, extolling the virtues of the Las Vegas highway strip, contends that the architect can be a "revolutionary" by adapting the palette of supermarkets, honky-tonks, gambling casinos, gas stations and parking lots to his work.*

How is such a view revolutionary? Well, most of Venturi's peers had been saying strip development is ugly and should be controlled, if not completely eliminated. Architects have been notoriously against commercial ugliness with its chaos

* "Learning from the existing landscape is a way of being revolutionary for an architect. . . . The Commercial Strip, the Las Vegas Strip in particular— it is the example par excellence—challenges the architect to take a positive, non-chip-on-the-shoulder view." (Venturi, Robert, and Brown, Denise Scott, "A Significance of A&P Parking Lots or Learning from Las Vegas," *Architectural Forum*, March 1968, p. 37.)

Robert Venturi, Architect

of product labels and its big neon signs, but in the liberal
tradition they are usually anti-commercialism rather than
anti-capitalist. That is, they fight the superficial effects of
the system rather than the system itself; they fight for
"progressive" zoning and "beautification" programs. Meanwhile, along comes Venturi and says all that stuff they've
been calling ugly is really beautiful! He tells us we're looking at the highway strip through the wrong set of theoretical
glasses. Wouldn't it be revolutionary if we suddenly saw as
beautiful all that stuff we've been calling ugly? That's obviously true, but what does such a distortion of our perception do to our larger view of the world? To be revolutionary
for the architect should mean something more than promoting a perversion of taste. It should involve a revolution
in the way people live; it means using architecture as a way
of breaking down the established social order. In this sense
Venturi's architecture is in fact the epitome of a counter-
revolutionary one. The real revolutionary architects are people like the squatters in Latin America. Faced with the
problem of a society where they own no land and need
homes, they make the act of designing and building their

170

own homes a political act of defiance against their social system.

Venturi instead takes the products of a sick social order (an order which he himself dislikes) and says that by aesthetically interpreting them as a new visual order outside the context of how they are used we can learn to enjoy them. What he doesn't do is go the next logical step in the argument. By learning to perceive this "garbage" through his new set of glasses, by giving it an aesthetic rationale, *the society is being immunized against the causes which produced the banalities in the first place*. Why bother to fight the capitalist interests that produce the blighted landscape when an architecture which assails your visual senses at every turn can be seen as "an architecture of bold communication rather than subtle persuasion"[25] (not bold persuasion, mind you, but "communication"). Why bother to question the values of the capitalist interests when you can convince yourself that

> The A&P parking lot is a current phase in the evolution of vast space since Versailles. . . . To move through this landscape is to move over vast expansive texture: the megatexture of the commercial landscape. The parking lot is the parterre of the asphalt landscape. The patterns, curbs, borders, and *tapis verts* give direction in Versailles: grids of lamp posts substitute for obelisks and rows of urns and statues, as points of identity and continuity in the vast space. But it is the highway signs through the sculptural forms or pictorial silhouettes, their particular positions in space, their inflected shapes, and their graphic meanings which identify and unify the megatexture. They make verbal and symbolic connections through space, communicating a complexity of meanings through hundreds of associations in a few seconds from far away.[26]

For all of Venturi's rhetoric about the "experience of life and the needs of society," his theory is a classic example of elitism. It is in the tradition of one architect producing a theory for the consumption of other architects and critics. It speaks to the tastemakers rather than to the needs of people (both poor and middle class) who are attempting to break a system which produces the grotesque environment they must now inhabit. It is an elite which can glorify the comic book or honky-tonk as something called "Pop." For they don't have to live that way—they don't read a comic book for its content, nor do they live in the banal environment of the "strip." They can appreciate its irony, its folksiness; they can intellectualize away the cause of these art forms by "discovering" (making an aesthetic of) its visual effect taken outside the context of its social reality.

> Las Vegas is analyzed here only as a phenomenon of architectural communication; its values are not questioned. Commercial advertising, gambling interests, and competitive instincts *are another matter*. The analysis of a drive-in church in this context would match that of a drive-in restaurant because *this is a study of method not content*.[27] (author's italics)

Just being able to isolate method and phenomenon from ideological content is in itself a disturbing and dangerous approach. Venturi's grotesque environmental results of abstracting method, disconnected for the purpose served by the method, recall all the more sharply Bakunin's warnings about allowing scientific endeavors to exist outside the bounds of those affected by this work. "In their present organization the monopolists of science," said the anarchist philosopher, "undoubtably form a separate caste which has much in common with the caste of priests. Scientific abstraction is their God, living and real individuals their victims, and they themselves the licensed and consecrated priests."[28]

By making the visual environment of the poor and lower middle class a phenomenon for stylish aesthetic titillation, isolated from the social values that produced this environment, it is easier for an intellectual elite to tolerate both the causes and the effects. What is normally considered

172

"ugly" has been analyzed and explained as a "good" method for producing architecture. It becomes a cultural phenomenon that can be seen in architectural books and art museums. You can study it in art-appreciation courses and you can talk about it at cocktail parties.

In a parallel way, an elite can relate to poverty by making it part of a full "social experience"; it becomes *another* part of one's daily existence to be dealt with, like what kind of clothes to buy for a coming party. "I had never seen a rat in my whole life until Gil and I went to see a day-care nursery in Anacostia," said the sophisticated wife of a Washington, D.C., politician, moving graciously between her concern for collecting pop art, planning a party for "important" people, choosing a new dress and helping put on an exhibit of the rat problem in a slum-neighborhood museum. "We went out on the children's playground and there was this huge rat. Now the Smithsonian's Anacostia Museum is going to have a rat show—the whole museum devoted to rats to show, without words, all about rats—and I'm helping them put it on." "How do I see myself?" she concluded. "As a contemporary person. And hopefully a lady."*

Elitist architecture now extends beyond the traditionally "aesthetic" or "visually" oriented planners like Venturi. Along with the increased professionalization of people's life

* Excerpted from the interview with Margot Hahn, *The New York Times*, August 9, 1969, p. 16.

"I'll buy my clothes in October. I need so many more daytime and cocktail dresses. For after 5 I like soft, crepey, covered-up, high neck, long sleeve things. I hope to get a long coat to wear over both miniskirts and trousers. . . .

"We gave a party recently for William (Turk) Thompson, the city councilman who has been appointed judge. Since he's from North Carolina, I thought I'd have a barbecue. We weren't Johnson people. But I thought it would jolly me. . . .

"I started buying these turn-of-the-century store machines when I stopped buying pop art. You've seen the match machine in the sitting room. It'll still give you a package of matches—saying Garfinckel's—if you put a penny in. . . .

"I go to all the council meetings and as many of the committee meetings as I can. The children are getting very interested in the city, too. It's what their father is about. . . ."

173

styles through architecture has come a new battery of social-science experts to help the architects. Complaining of the traditional architects' intuitive approach untested by the experimental method, these experts have called for more "scientific" information about the way people use space. For some architects, teaming up with social scientists or using their "data" is seen as a way to resolve the contradiction of dealing with the building's financial developer, instead of the people who actually use the buildings. But the use of "data" is at best a way of ameliorating the contradiction rather than resolving it. At worst it can lead to some dangerous conclusions about how places should be designed.

OBSERVATION, IDEOLOGY AND CULTURE

Supported by a $90,000 federal grant from the Water Pollution Control Administration, the state's Department of Sea and Shore Fisheries will warm the Atlantic Ocean and build mass housing projects for lobsters in an effort to increase the declining crustacean population.

Robert L. Dow, research director of the department, said an area in Casco Bay will be warmed by water discharged from the Central Maine Power Company plant at Yarmouth.

Lobsters grow faster in warmer temperatures, said Dow.

"We plan to build mass housing projects using various types of shelter material on the bottom to protect the lobsters from predators," Dow explained.

"At the same time, we also plan to design and develop plastic encapsulating shelters which will further protect the crustacean and also reduce differences in water temperatures," Dow added. . . .

"By using air curtains, we plan to mix the warm thermal discharge with the colder winter water and prolong lobster activity, reduce the hibernation period, and get quicker molts. We feel sure it can be done," said Dow.

—Boston *Globe*[29]

174

A potent example of the "scientific" approach to architecture is the work of Edward T. Hall, an anthropologist who has gained favor, especially among some of the younger architects. At least part of his welcome lies no doubt in his being one of the first social scientists to describe the architectural implications of his observations.

Drawing on the pioneering linguistic work of anthropologist Franz Boas and linguists Edward Sapir and Benjamin Lee Whorf, he begins with the hypothesis that people from different cultures not only perceive and use the same words differently, but also perceive and use environmental space differently.[30] Discussing these ideas, he has indeed made some accurate observations. The difference between the way Japanese and Americans use space is especially interesting. Says Hall:

> In the use of interior space, the Japanese keep the edges of their rooms clear because everything takes place in the middle. Europeans tend to fill up the edges by placing furniture near or against the walls. As a consequence, Western rooms often look less cluttered to the Japanese than they do to us.[31]

> In Japan . . . the walls are movable, opening and closing as the day's activities change. In the United States, people move from room to room or from one part of a room to another for each different activity, such as eating, sleeping, working, or socializing with relatives. In Japan, it is quite common for the person to remain in one spot while the activities change.[32]*

* Unfortunately, in the midst of such descriptions Hall moves on to a bit of pseudo-science. Describing how crowding induces stress in people, Hall notes,

> Like gravity, the influence of two bodies on each other is inversely proportional not only to the square of the distance but possibly even the cube of the distance between them. When stress increases, sensitivity to crowding rises—people get more on edge—so that more and more space is required as less and less is available. (P. 129.)

That people under stress would be sensitive to crowding is good common sense indeed. That there is anything like the laws of gravity or an inversely proportional mathematical relationship involved in all this would seem to ask for some data supporting his observation; none is given.

Hall's observations, such as the difference between Japanese and American perceptions, open new possibilities for people to use and enjoy space. But these are not the lessons we are supposed to learn. Hall sees these studies enabling city planners and architects to design more socially controllable cities—planners as soft cops with a law-and-order program through environmental design.

"The lower-class Negro in the United States," says Hall, "poses very special problems in his adjustment to city living, which if they are not solved may well destroy us by making our cities uninhabitable."[33] To solve this, city planners should create

> . . . congenial spaces that will encourage and strengthen the cultural enclave. This will serve two purposes: first, it will assist the city and the enclave in the transformation process that takes place generation by generation as country folk are converted to city dwellers; and second, it will strengthen social controls that combat lawlessness.[34]

Neither the purpose of this "transformation process" nor the nature of "lawlessness" are questioned. What is tacitly accepted is the "conversion" of "country folk" by the planners, rather than a process determined by the people themselves. As for "lawlessness," Hall makes no distinction between justifiable and non-justifiable disobedience of the laws. Should rebelling against your oppression be considered lawlessness or sanity? These are presumably unfit questions for a "scientific" investigation. The planners' job, as we will see, is to make the situation of the oppressed tolerable by keeping them healthy. Says Hall:

> According to a recent *Time* report, 232,000 people are packed into three and half square miles in Harlem. Apart from letting the sink run its course and destroy the city, there is an alternative solution: *introduce design features that will counteract the ill effects of the sink but not destroy the enclave in the process.* In animal populations, the solution is simple enough and frighteningly like what

176

we seen in our urban renewal programs as well as our
suburban sprawl. To increase density in a rat population
and maintain healthy specimens, put them in boxes so
they can't see each other, clean their cages, and give them
enough to eat. You can pile the boxes up as many stories as
you wish. Unfortunately, caged animals become stupid,
which is a very heavy price to pay for a super filing system! The question we must ask ourselves is, How far can
we afford to travel down the road of sensory deprivation
in order to file people away? One of man's most critical
needs, therefore, is for principles for designing spaces
that will maintain a healthy density, a healthy interaction
rate, a proper amount of involvement, and a continuing
sense of ethnic identification. The creation of such principles will require the combined efforts of many diverse
specialists all working closely together on a massive
scale.[35]

There are no moral questions in this "scientific" approach.
The question is related to health—the inhabitants must not
become stupid, there must be a "healthy density" and "interaction rate," a "proper amount of involvement." In the
expert game, one has to couch reform in the expert language. That it is simply immoral to make people live in a
filing system isn't enough—one must attack it on scientific
grounds. One must be able to show what happens to rats who
live this way to make it seem reasonable to change it for
human beings. And then the professionals must take it upon
themselves, working through some "massive" framework, to
make the change (the "many diverse specialists all working
closely together on a massive scale").

As for the kind of environment Hall finds appropriate, he
points to Marina City, two circular apartment buildings
(filing cabinets indeed) for higher-income families on the
edge of the Chicago River. According to Hall, Marina City
has

> . . . features that answer the needs of the city dwellers:
> restaurant, bar and taverns, a supermarket, liquor store,

Marina Towers, Chicago

theater, ice skating rink, a bank, boat basins, and even an art gallery. It is safe, protected from weather and possible city violence (you don't need to go outside for anything).[36] (Hall's parenthesis)

"Restaurant, bar and taverns, a supermarket, liquor store, theater, ice skating rink, a bank, boat basins, and even an art gallery"—what more could you ask for? Maybe a Chinese restaurant, a pizza place and a cemetery, and people would really be able to stay inside forever, safe from the world around them. And presumably Hall would like to keep our world this way, since the message of this book, as he states it, is that man and his culture are inseparable. "In the briefest possible sense," says Hall, "the message of this book is that no matter how hard man tries, it is impossible to divest himself of his own culture, for it has penetrated to the roots of his nervous system and determines how he perceives the world."[37]

We professionals, charged with designing the environment, must regard these cultural constraints in our designs. Anthropologists and psychologists will collect data for us which will measure the amount of sensory involvement that people in different cultural groups have with each other— what Hall calls their "involvement ratios." According to Hall:

> The degree to which peoples are sensorially involved with each other, and how they use time, determine not only at what point they are crowded but the methods for relieving crowding as well. Puerto Ricans and Negroes have a

R. Buckminster Fuller, Proposal for Harlem, N.Y.

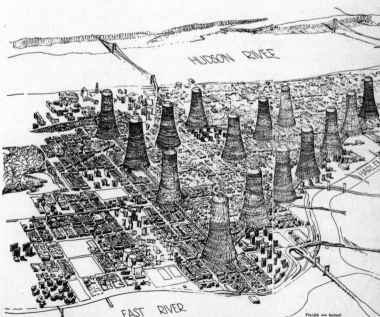

New city proposal by Paolo Soleri. (Note scale of Empire State Building at left.)

much higher involvement ratio than New Englanders and Americans of German or Scandinavian stock. Highly involved people apparently require higher densities than less involved people, and they may also require more protection or screening from outsiders. It is absolutely essential that we learn more about how to compute the maximum, minimum, and optimum density of the different cultural enclaves that make up our cities.[38]

The fact that a cultural group now uses its environment in some way is hardly a sufficient basis for drawing conclusions about the kind of places that would be right for the group. People often behave in certain predictable ways because they are constrained by their social and physical environment from behaving otherwise. To rigidify and institutionalize the environments different cultural groups now use could simply mean making more permanent the repression that has been built into their culture. Architect Venturi, for example, uses what he considers the cultural traits of Americans to justify our enlightened continuity with the status quo. Arguing against the compulsive use of outdoor plazas in recent American planning, he says, "Americans feel uncomfortable sitting in a square. They should be working at the office or at home with the family looking at television."[39] It's true that modern architects have not understood how people *could* use urban open spaces and have left vast unusable areas in our cities (much like the A&P parking lots that Venturi is so enamored of). But to argue against city squares and in favor of more isolated experience on the basis of present American cultural traits is hardly an answer to the problem of alienation of people from each other in this country.

The logical conclusion of Hall's own observations further illustrates the danger of considering culture as a static phenomenon. "Middle Eastern subjects in public places," he says, "do not express the outraged reaction to being touched by strangers which one encounters in American subjects."[40]

If one accepts Hall's cultural-inevitability theory, one would build these biases into the social or physical system of each culture. Americans would be given more room in public places to keep them from being touched. But the fact that Americans are afraid to be touched is at least as much part of how people have been trained at home, in their schools and their jobs, which are, after all, extensions of their political and economic institutions. While you can describe it as a cultural trait, you can't deny that revolution in different parts of the world has been able to change political and economic institutions which in turn are capable of changing these traits. It is hardly any more inevitable that Chinese, North Vietnamese and Cubans are socialist and have developed cooperative institutions than it is inevitable that Americans are capitalists and competitive. If what has been called the "counter culture" in this country has proved anything, it's just the opposite of cultural inevitability.

This is hardly to argue against the existence of distinct traits in different cultures. But it does show the kind of subtle and dangerous repression which can occur if we accept a so-called scientific view of cultural inevitability as a substitute for a political and moral analysis of why cultural groups behave as they do. It's this sort of pseudo-science that tacitly accepts the present political system and leads some social scientists to the conclusion that blacks, owing to their cultural background, aren't able to do as well educationally as whites.

But architects are relatively new to the game of using "scientific" data to justify their subjective and often politically inspired conclusions. City planners, on the other hand, have been practicing this kind of science for many years. To understand this tradition, let us look back again to the factory camp city at the turn of the century.

182

VI

The Scientific
Method: Salvation
from Politics

Technology can be used to subjugate the people or it can be
used to liberate them. . . . And whoever says that a tech-
nician of whatever sort, be he an architect, doctor, engineer,
scientist, etc., needs solely to work with his instruments, in
his chosen specialty, while his countrymen are starving or
wearing themselves out in the struggle, has de facto gone
over to the other side. He is not apolitical: he has taken a
political decision, but one opposed to the movements for
liberation. . . .
>   —Che Guevara, International Union of Architects
>   (UIA) Congress, Havana, 1963

AS A FACTORY CAMP, the nineteenth-century city could be
tolerated by the upper classes so long as their sensibilities
weren't offended. But as escape from the visual and social
chaos became more difficult, as competition among big business was seen by them as self-destructive and inefficient, and
as the slums couldn't insure a healthy worker population,
then incentives were strong for the upper classes to revise
the rules of their "gentlemen's agreement" for real-estate
development; that is, as long as rewriting the rules could be
rationalized to them as supporting their own interests.

Arguing for city planning at the first National Conference on City Planning in 1909, Robert Anderson Pope, a landscape architect, claimed:

> . . . city planning through removing the laboring classes from the congested districts promotes industrial efficiency. This increased efficiency comes from the greater health that the ample sunshine and the fresh air which is secured to the city; the greater health that results from contentment with the more attractive surroundings with their trees, their flowers, and their playgrounds . . . for in the final accounting does not their [the upper classes] prosperity depend upon that of the lower classes?[1]

More than half a century later, President Lyndon B. Johnson, considered a liberal on domestic programs, would raise the same rationalizations for improving the "factory camp." "Cities are the places where the labor force lives," he told a group of businessmen, academics and government officials, "where they must rely on systems of urban transportation to travel to and from work. Cities are the places where the chaos or serenity of the worker's environment affects his productivity and morale. The city is the great and complex organization in which business and production must be carried out. If the city is inefficient, doing business is inefficient and costly."[2]

With increased immigrant population in the early 1900s the lower classes had become a dominant political force in the city. From the perspective of the established urban groups, landowners and factory owners, the lower-class immigrants were taking not only political control but economic control as well. Of course, big business and the large institutions did their share of slum building and management (in 1894, Trinity Church was the single largest owner of tenement property in New York City).[3] But the system had also in effect been open to exploitation by new groups. You could make money in America—you had to learn the system, sweat for some investment money and then do your own exploitation. This is what some sociologists called the immigrants' "upward mobility." A study of the housing reform movement notes:

> The *New York Times,* after a survey in 1896, concluded that "the tenements and the rear tenements in this city are very largely, almost entirely, owned by people of moderate means in the 'middle classes' of the community." Half the rear tenements were "owned by individuals, both men and women, who themselves live in their miserable premises." The *Times* published the names of the owners of all the rear tenements in the city and judging from these names many of the owners were German, Irish, Jewish and Italian immigrants or their descendants. A later survey of property distribution on the lower East Side revealed that for a sample parcel of holdings in January 1900 less than $500,000 in value, 72.8 percent were owned by individuals in contrast to "estates, corporations and other combinations."[4]

The big landowners and real-estate developers needed "protection" against such free market operators and the blight that accompanied their dealings.[5] No district was safe from the effects of the free and enterprising newcomers. Banks holding mortgages in potentially exploitable areas feared for their investments; owners of property in well-to-do areas feared the riff-raff that might move next door to their high-rent-paying tenants. Restrictions on property were an economic necessity for the large business interests. Radical economic and political theoreticians and organizers could speak about the need to nationalize land so that the value earned by public improvement and development would be shared by the community. But the advent of city planning, with its power to regulate land development with such tools as zoning, came not as the answer to the radical's demand for government ownership of land but as the victory of one group of entrenched business interests over another. The reformers' call for "good government," meaning people with "professional" know-how replacing political favorites, fell on friendly ears in the business world. Lincoln Steffens, one of this "Progressive Era's" most famous reformers, could hardly be considered to have antagonized business with his call for "law and order" as a protection against striking workers. Chicago, complained Steffens, had a police force "so insufficient (and inefficient) that it cannot protect itself, to say nothing of handling mobs, riotous strikers, and the rest of that lawlessness which disgraces Chicago."[6] Good government meant that people with more "substance" and the "proper" background and values should take over the responsibility of running the city.[7]

In 1909 the secretary of the Cleveland Chamber of Commerce told the country's First National Conference on City Planning:

> It seems obvious that big city undertakings should be initiated and urged by the *men who have the imagination to conceive large private enterprises* and the ability to carry them through successfully. These are the men whose interest in this work should be enlisted and whose good judgment should govern their direction. . . . Until the day shall arrive when *men of that character* are willing to devote their time to the public good by serving in public office, so long as the initiative for great public improvements must come from without rather than from within the minds of city officials, it seems to me that those organizations which are composed of the *business and professional men, the men of means and influence and leisure,* are the organizations from whom we should expect wise and progressive city planning.[8] (author's italics)

"Politics" in the turn-of-the-century factory camp was considered by many reformers a necessary, but often evil, process—a process which bred on the social chaos of the city, the immigrants, the poor and the uneducated. The representative democracy called for by the Constitution could be tolerated at a time when only an educated elite, for the most part, took part in politics. When masses of "less desirable" people became involved, then politics, in the reformers' eyes, became corrupt. In their view, City Hall was filled with the wrong political friends, and the wrong political machines ran the city. City planning thus became (as it continues to be) the equivalent of the "white man's burden." The elite, the responsible, those with moral conscience had to promote the interests of the poor, who supposedly didn't know any better. It wasn't a radical political and economic adjustment that was necessary, but a "moral awakening" of those in power. Addressing the 1909 conference, Henry Morgenthau, patting himself and his colleagues on the back, stated:

> To those who have long labored to ameliorate the conditions of those who are forced to live as best they can, not as they should or would like it, it is indeed most encouraging to have the *foremost* citizens of our community approve of those endeavors. It is but another proof of the greatness of this country that *these highest in power* give heed to the wants of the least favored of the land. The civic endeavors of *the intelligent part of our community* aim at greatest efficiency, and the planning is essential to such efficiency. We have had a moral awakening, and are ready and anxious to do our duty. We are all proud of our country, its achievements, and the opportunities it has offered us and is offering others. We will not permit anything to mar its onward progress, if we can help it.[9] (author's italics)

MAKING IT LEGAL

Zoning can protect you against the small, inefficient entrepreneur. Zoning can protect the big fellow against the marauding of little guys who have nothing at all in mind.
          —John E. Burchard, architectural historian and former Dean of MIT's School of Humanities and Social Sciences, to a group of large real-estate developers, architects and city planners.[10]

187

If a more workable factory camp was to be achieved, the techniques of ameliorating its worst excesses and rationalizing it as an architectural form would have to be acceptable to the "gentlemen" with a financial interest in land. An owner's right to use his property for profit was a formidable historic tradition, supported legally by state governments and the Fifth and Fourteenth Amendments of the United States Constitution. A city could, of course, condemn property by using its eminent-domain powers and pay for it—but that would not be acceptable to the "property interests." As the Commission on the Height of Buildings, one of the earliest groups interested in zoning, advised the New York City government in 1913:

> It is theoretically conceivable that a general plan of building restriction and regulation might be entered upon by resort to the power of eminent domain, but practically, such a resolution is out of the question. The expense and

burden of condemnation proceedings and litigation in mul-
titudinous cases could create a tax burden that would increase rather than compensate for the injury to property
interests.[11]

The support of such reasoning by the courts made zoning
the single most important tool in the planners' trade for
many years. It would take planning out of the "visionary"
stage, giving it a legal foothold for controlling land development. It would let government regulate the use of land without requiring the government to pay an owner for the loss of
his development potential.

The established business interests increasingly gave much
of the important support for zoning, a phenomenon not so
surprising as it may first appear. Zoning might put controls
on entrepreneurs' abilities to develop their land in whatever
way they wished, but even more importantly it could stabi-
lize and increase property values. Edward M. Bassett, a
lawyer and inventor of zoning (often called the "Father of
City Planning"), argued:

> It may seem paradoxical to hold that a policy of building
> restriction tends to a fuller utilization of land than a
> policy of no restriction; but such is undoubtedly the case.
> The reason lies in the greater safety and security to in-
> vestment secured by definite restriction.[12]

That the restrictions city planning's father created could
in fact be used to manipulate land values to the owner's
advantage was a feature not lost on real-estate owners. In a
trade-off between unlimited freedom and stabilization of
value, businessmen would have better reason to see profit in
the latter. In commercial, industrial and apartment areas
zoning would generally call for more development than
developers would ever ask for.[13] In 1939, according to New
York's zoning code, the city could provide enough business
and industrial space for a city of 340 million[14] and in 1959
it allowed enough residential space for 55 million.[15] Bos-

ton's 1924 zoning ordinance allowed industrial development on 25 percent of the city's land although only 2½ percent was used for industry at that time.[16]

Zoning was justified by its supporters on the basis that it would protect a community's "health," "safety," "morals," "general welfare" and "property values," but it was the latter that garnered its greatest support. A 1953 court case succinctly stated the property-oriented bias of the "general welfare" jargon of the zoners.

> . . . in order to be valid, zoning restrictions and limitations must have a tendency to promote the general welfare by prohibiting in particular areas uses which would be detrimental to the full enjoyment of the established use of the property in that area. *The real object, however, of promoting the general welfare by zoning ordinances is to protect the private use and enjoyment of property and to promote the welfare of the individual property owner. In other words, promoting the general welfare is a means of protecting private property.*[17] (author's italics)

With zoning, the businessmen could have their cake and eat it too; the "character" of the neighborhoods where they lived would be maintained while they could reap enormous profits from the neighborhoods of those they exploited. It could also be used to promote such general welfare as making sure where certain kinds of people could live or not live. The first case of zoning in this country was a tragic example of this tradition. In 1885, San Francisco created an ordinance eliminating Chinese laundries in sections of the city, putting three hundred laundries out of business overnight. The California courts, which had earlier struck down a blatant attempt at direct discrimination, went on to uphold the legality of this law.[18] Thus, an "end run" model for legal discrimination through zoning had been established.

While the courts have usually struck down clear-cut cases of using zoning to discriminate, the ways of zoning are not always so clearly cut. Large-lot zoning, which effectively

191

excludes the poor by increasing the cost of house lots, can be used in suburbs to maintain "neighborhood character." An important question to ponder is whose morals, health, safety and general welfare are being protected by zoning for two-acre lots in certain areas of the city and one-quarter-acre lots in another.

Zoning can also be used by real-estate developers who want the opportunity for extensive "high density" or apartment-house zoning in the parts of the city where they own land. By operating either as politicians themselves, or through their positions on zoning boards, or through friendly politicians, these developers can obtain changes in zoning maps or "zoning variances" to favor their own interests.

INTEGRATION, THE PLANNERS AND THE POOR

Addressing the problem of racial discrimination, planners and reformers have proposed their now traditional answer of government-enforced integration. In housing, for example, more "mixed" zoning would give the poor, especially blacks, greater access to housing, jobs and schools in the suburbs.[19] But the perverse result of such reforms would be simply to impose on the suburbs the same "low cost" environmental blight that now exists in the center city. The problem with the suburbs, as with the rest of the country, is not their lack of low-income housing or their homogeneous character; it's that one class of people can live in an environment with certain "character" of *their* choosing, while the mass of the population has this character determined by the economics of real-estate exploitation. Such exploitation can take direct forms, such as maintaining slums, or it can take more subtle forms of molding people's opinions about the joys of the suburban ranch house. But the answer to this isn't spreading the blight of low-income projects to the

192

suburbs; it lies in creating situations where all people are economically and psychically liberated to come together and determine the character of their neighborhoods—whether it be "homogeneous" or "mixed."

To move in the direction of liberal zoning reform is to move into the same morass the liberals created in their drive for integrated schools, the result of which has been mainly to increase racial tensions. Forced zoning integration of the suburbs will further aggravate racial antagonisms of up-ward-striving poor whites who struggled to make it into the promised land of the subdivision. The areas that will likely become available for such housing will be the lower-income sections of the suburbs, not the executive estates. The wealthy property owners can afford to hold their land, but the smaller developers will be induced to sell as the value of their land increases when its zoning is changed from single-family to apartment housing. The newly arriving blacks who will live in the project-type housing allowed by liberal zoning will be seen by the whites as the cause of the "char-acter" of their area changing from more rural to less rural.

In this same sense, liberals created tension between work-ing-class whites and blacks by pressing for such reforms as integrated schools. Social integration in the absence of eco-nomic equality simply put low-income people in a more intense struggle with each other for welfare crumbs. Working-class whites are rightly angered when welfare programs, Model City legislation, scholarships are determined on a racial basis. The white workers are the ones who feel the tax increases for welfare programs; their children are forced to be bussed to decrepit schools in black areas; job-hiring policies put black workers ahead of them; and their children have less chance for college scholarships.

While liberals tried helping blacks by moralizing about "the evils of racism," they neglected the analysis of the economic conditions which promoted such racism. Rather than exposing how schools, for example, were channeling both white and black students toward acceptable roles for a capitalist economy, their proposals emphasized preferential treatment of an isolated, specially defined "underprivileged" group. If problems can be isolated and cared for on cultural or "underprivileged" bases, the assumption remains that the rest of the population is privileged. The questionable substance of such privileges notwithstanding, the "privileged" groups see the meager privileges they have or are striving for being eroded. The "underprivileged" group (the blacks) reaping the benefits, and "big government," which in essence acts in the interest of the corporations, become their enemy. Racist candidates like George Wallace, playing on the fears of the marginally privileged, become attractive alternatives for the "little man" fighting big government.

". . . COORDINATED, ADJUSTED AND HARMONIOUS DEVELOPMENT . . ."

Herbert Hoover, a man not often portrayed as a staunch advocate of government control of private enterprise, played what may seem a surprising role in gaining government control of planning. But judging from the benefits to business from zoning and planning, Hoover's leadership in bringing government into the process is understandable. Before the 1920s, city planning had been carried out for the most part directly by private benefactors and civic improvement associations run by local business interests. These groups organized themselves to lobby with city governments and "educate" the public with proposals and studies. Influencing the movement toward governmentalizing city-planning operations were two documents prepared by the federal government under Hoover's guidance, then head of the Department of Commerce: the Standard State Zoning Enabling Act of 1924 and the Standard City Planning Enabling Act of 1928* These documents suggested the legal nomenclature for states to give their cities the right to zone and plan.

The zoning guide was meant to formalize legal technique already in practice. Hoover's city-planning guide, calling for the local non-elected city-planning commission, would further remove power to control land development from the disenfranchised city groups—the tenants, the poor and those without property. The vaguely worded guidelines, when adopted by the states, would give cities broad legal powers to use city planning. It stated that a city plan

> . . . shall be made with the general purpose of guiding and accomplishing a *coordinated, adjusted and harmonious development* of the municipality and its environs which will, in accordance with present and future needs, best promote *health, safety, morals, order, convenience, prosperity and general welfare,* as well as *efficiency and economy in the process of development.*[20] (author's italics)

* The Hoover report, outlining extraordinary powers of development control for planning commissions, suggested that these powers be vested in a primarily non-elected board. "The report suggested the commission be comprised of nine members, including the mayor, a council member, a current city administrative official appointed by the mayor, and six people appointed by the mayor. The term for the six appointees was six years, while the positions of the administrative official would terminate when the mayor left office." After the commission adapts a plan, suggests the report, "no street, square, park or other public way, ground, or open space, or public building or structure, or public utility, whether publicly or privately owned, shall be contracted or authorized in the municipality or in such planned section and district until the location, character, and extent thereof shall have been submitted to and approved by the commission. . . ."

195

While the guidelines allowed overruling of the commission by the council, it called for a two-thirds vote—in effect, reducing the power of a small neighborhood to control its own land development. More important, though, it gave the council, the city's elected board, only a negative way to approach community development: its members could disapprove plans but they couldn't initiate action. It effectively cut off political representatives from direct control of planning.

It was independence from both the administrative and legislative branches that Hoover's group sought for the planning arm of the government.* The excuse for divorcing planning from the council's control was the supposed predictive nature of the planning board's work. Crystal-ball gazing could be entrusted only to politically disinterested people —in the words of the guidelines, the board should be

> . . . free from the pressure of purely current problems. Consequently, the council, by virtue of its term of office, does not have the qualification, the time, or the *political status* which would make it an appropriate body for this long-time planning work.[21] (author's italics)

How being *appointed* rather than *elected* gave the specially chosen planning board the political status required to make decisions that would affect the lives of individuals in a community for years to come was never discussed by the Hoover report. But if the guidelines were vague on this point, they were certain to suggest the representation of business owners on the planning commission, even by people living outside the community. It stated that the

> . . . requirement that these citizens (the board) shall be

* "Planning is just as important and essential a function of city government as is administration or legislation. In other words, the successful and efficient work of city government, for the promotion of the public health, convenience, safety, and welfare, requires the exercise of three distinct functions of planning, legislation, and administration, each in charge of separate officers or boards. The planning board is that organ of the municipal government which performs this planning function, and within its sphere it needs *the same independence, specialized qualification, and permanence as the other organs of the city government need in their respective spheres.*" (author's italics)

electors of the particular municipality is not recommended, for often a person who is well adapted for this kind of service resides in some nearby suburb and *has large business interests* in the municipality in question.[22] (author's italics)

THE PUBLIC INTEREST THROUGH SCIENTIFIC MANAGEMENT

You may very appropriately want to ask me how we are going to resolve the ever-accelerating dangerous impasse of world-opposed politicians and ideological dogmas. I answer, it will be resolved by the computer. Man has ever-increasing confidence in the computer; witness his unconcerned landings as airtransport passengers coming in for a landing in the combined invisibility of fog and night. While no politician or political system can ever afford to yield understandably and enthusiastically to their adversaries and opposers, all politicians can and will yield enthusiastically to the computers safe flight-controlling capabilities in bringing all of humanity in for a happy landing.

So, planners, architects, and engineers take the initiative. Go to work, and above all co-operate and don't hold back on one another or try to gain at the expense of another.[23]

—R. Buckminster Fuller

By 1937 there were only two states without some form of legislation giving cities the legal right to plan. With what the planners began to call "comprehensive planning," the poor, who traditionally had little access to power, were going to have even less. The planning of cities was to be entrusted to professionals, who would supposedly consider all interests of the city in their objective, scientific, non-political analyses and then arrive at a "comprehensive plan." In this best of all possible worlds, answering to the illusive goal of promoting the general welfare, everyone would supposedly give and receive his fair share of the planning pie.

In 1939 Rexford Tugwell, then chairman of New York

197

City's Planning Commission, made what is perhaps the classic case for such scientific planning. In a speech to a meeting of city planners, Tugwell, who was later to become one of Franklin D. Roosevelt's closest advisers, called for a separate branch of the federal government staffed by planning experts that would be on a par with the executive, the legislative and the judicial branches.[24] It was to be called the "directive" branch and charged with determining "social policy" for the country.[25] His argument is interesting, not so much for this specific proposal as for the fact that it is a classic vision of the expert as free from politics, scientifically working in the interest of everyone.

Tugwell was unclear about how people would become part of this branch, except to say they "ought to be given longer-term appointments than any other except judicial officials. . . ."[26] The directive would differ basically from the other branches in that it would deal with "fact" rather than special political interests or legal precedents or organizational problems. The expert's devotion to fact and scientific forecasting techniques was to offer people protection against the persons using the directive branch for political gain. Tugwell's views on this bear some lengthy quotation.

> The margin of safety which the community possesses in entrusting power to the directive is widened by its persistent orientation to the future, a future discovered by charting the trends of the past through the present. And this projection is not subject to opinion or to change as a result of pressure from special interests. In this forecasting of the shape of things to come, it can succeed, aside from maintaining the most honorable relation with facts, only by possessing and using the most modern techniques for discovering them. It thus has an interest in progress and in modernization which is quite different from the traditional interests of the other powers. The discipline of fact is a more impressive one than the discipline of legal ethics or even a watchful constituency. . . . It may thus establish a genuinely social policy, as contrasted with

private policies, dictated by contemporary resources, techniques and circumstances, rather than by political expediency; tuned to the universe, the continent, the region, and the times, rather than to an imaginary environment in some past utopia for speculators in private advantage. It will not be pursued because it suits a whim, a prejudice, an economic interest or a political gain. It will be distilled with modern devices from the then controlling conditions for the success of society. It will take account of all there is to work with and allow itself to be guided only by the interests of all there are to work for.[27]

As a dream, it is not without imagination. It is similar to the argument used by experts to stress their "objective," "non-ideological" position. As a projected reality of a scientific priest class, untouched by our earthly political considerations, gathering data and charting the future for everyone, it bears some scrutiny. What Tugwell failed to mention is that the experts do in fact operate from an ideological or value position, and their so-called unbiased technical answers reflect this. Even the choice of what's to be studied, what trends they decide to project, involves considering one set of concerns that seem important and rejecting others that are supposedly not important. The generalization that the "discipline of fact is a more impressive one than the discipline of legal ethics or a watchful constituency" is not only absurd but misleading. The problem is hardly that facts are more important than legal ethics or a watchful constituency. The problem is that facts can't be separated from a particular set of ethics (legal or otherwise) and the constituency they serve.

In a sense, facts are value free so long as nobody sees or uses them. But as soon as they're put together to support or reject a particular position, the facts become part of that position. The problem then is what set of moral ethics, what "position," should facts be used to support. Positions must be determined by asking such questions as "Is it *morally* right for all people to share equally the nation's resources, or should some have more and some have less?" "Is it *morally* acceptable to kill people in another country in order to maintain our economic interests there?" etc.

Obviously, different experts will have different opinions on these ideological issues. And equally obviously, those in power will seek out those experts whose ideological position is similar to their own and who will support this position with "facts." By giving directive power to the experts in a separate branch of government hardly means they're going to be guided only by everyone's interest. This is an obvious impossibility in a system where, for example, the interest of the corporation owner is quite different from that of the worker.

To Tugwell's credit, he had a clear perception of the dangers of planning tools if misdirected. "Scientific management, interchangeable parts and series operations were, in other words," he said, "such inventions in other fields as the airplane which now drops bombs on its inventors."[28] He admitted that planning was "a process unfamiliar, even uncongenial to the American habit." In this process

. . . the individual can no longer exercise his initiative in a manner which affects a large industry or a planned city. The processes of change are reduced to an order in which the individual, except as a member of the cooperating whole, cannot be allowed to function freely, if at all. *Others think out problems which affect the individual.*[29] (author's italics)

But for this enormous dilemma Tugwell had little to say, except to propose that planners would find answers through the "experimental method" and that they not be dissuaded from their task by "rampant individualists" who "belong to the past and not the future; and [who] are likely to die out, moreover, through lack of adaptation."[30] He was probably referring to big-businessmen. But alas, the evolution of planning hardly did them in. The people in danger and those bearing the brunt of the planners' programs were hardly the big-businessmen. Not only have these businessmen adapted, but indeed Tugwell's planning experts, immersed in fact, have been just the ones who helped this come about.

ENTER THE TECHNOCRATS

For the liberals of the 1950s and 1960s, Tugwell's model of planning as a "scientific" process removed from the subjective vagaries of politics, had become a super image in government, not simply as a fourth power but replacing other powers as well. Rationalism of the professional was seen as the objective substitute for the self-interest of the politician. Daniel Bell, a well-known liberal political theoretician, wrote, "The tendency to convert concrete issues into ideological problems, to invest them with moral color, is to invite conflicts which can only damage a society."[31]

When John F. Kennedy became President, he was to echo a similar theme:

> What is at stake in our economic decisions today is not some grand warfare of rival ideologies which will sweep the country with passion, but the practical management of a modern economy. What we need are not labels and clichés but more basic discussion of the sophisticated and technical questions involved in keeping a great economic machinery moving ahead. . . .
>
> I am suggesting that the problems of fiscal and monetary policy in the Sixties as opposed to the kinds of problems we faced in the Thirties demand subtle challenges for which technical answers—not political answers—must be provided.[32]

So did his New Frontier Secretary of Housing and Urban Development (HUD), Robert C. Weaver. In the position he maintained under Lyndon B. Johnson, Weaver noted:

> Today, concern over issues has given way to concern for

201

broad problems. As contemporary problems such as poverty, social disorganization, civil rights and rampant urbanization become readily identified, Creative Federalism [Johnson's ideological nomenclature] responds with solutions instead of ideologies.[33]

In his role as New Frontier (Kennedy's ideological nomenclature) leader, Kennedy would bring a special breed of technocrats to government. Often brimming over with the language of reason and science, they served the cause of some of the most regressive political policies the world has seen. Said one New Frontiersman:

Some critics today worry that our democratic, free societies are becoming overmanaged. I would argue that the opposite is true. As paradoxical as it may sound, the real threat to democracy comes, not from overmanagement, but from undermanagement. To undermanage reality is not to keep free. It is simply to let some force other than reason shape reality. That force may be unbridled emotion; it may be greed; it may be aggressiveness; it may be hatred; it may be ignorance; it may be inertia; it may be anything other than reason. But whatever it is, if it is not reason that rules man, then man falls short of his potential.

Vital decision-making, particularly in policy matters, must remain at the top. This is partly, though not completely, what the top is for. But rational decision-making depends on having a full range of rational options from which to choose, and successful management organizes the enterprise so that process can best take place. It is a mechanism whereby free men can most efficiently exercise their reason, initiative, creativity and personal responsibility. The adventurous and immensely satisfying task of an efficient organization is to formulate and analyze these options.[34]

That was former Secretary of Defense Robert S. McNamara, Kennedy's and Johnson's "rational" manager of the wars in Vietnam and other parts of the world.

On the domestic front, there were Kennedy's urban experts diagnosing the ills of society and bringing forth a multitude of programs. Epitomizing the planner as rational scientist on this front was Daniel P. Moynihan, who served under Kennedy as Assistant Secretary of Labor and later as Richard M. Nixon's chief adviser on urban problems. While some liberals have criticized Moynihan for this double allegiance, by Moynihan's own definition of the expert he really didn't have much of a problem. For Moynihan, the planner is a kind of urban doctor, and doctors obviously can heal anyone without concern for political beliefs. As head of

203

Harvard and MIT's Joint Center for Urban Studies, he was once asked by a reporter why a $6 million Ford Foundation grant was given to these universities to establish chairs in urban studies rather than to a low-income neighborhood to develop its own program. Said Moynihan, "We should not like to suggest that we are anything but immensely grateful to the Ford Foundation, but, sir, quite, really, you know, would you say you can rephrase your question and ask *why do you spend money on cancer research when you could give money to people who had cancer?*"[35] (author's italics)

Behind the attitude is Moynihan's elitist belief that the poor, having no way of declaring their poverty, are helpless to do anything about their problems until the politicians, led by the urban doctors, come to their rescue. "The poor of Appalachia were not only 'invisible' but silent as well," said Moynihan. The poverty program was declared not "at the behest of the poor; it was declared in their interest by persons confident of their own judgment in such matters."[36] The provision of the 1964 Poverty Program that called for "maximum feasible participation of the poor" originated, according to Moynihan, with the professionals. "The point being," said Moynihan, "that professional persons made professional judgments that the poor should be involved. That is what the professions do: they know best."[37]

With the patient not knowing what ails him, the doctor's job, according to Moynihan, is to get the treatment going without bothering to tell the patient what his problem is all about.

His [Kennedy's] election brought to Washington as office holders, or consultants, or just friends, a striking echelon of persons whose profession might justifiably be described as *knowing what ails societies* and whose art it is to get treatment under way before the *patient* is especially aware of anything noteworthy taking place.[38] (author's italics)

In this position Moynihan has ample support from one of

204

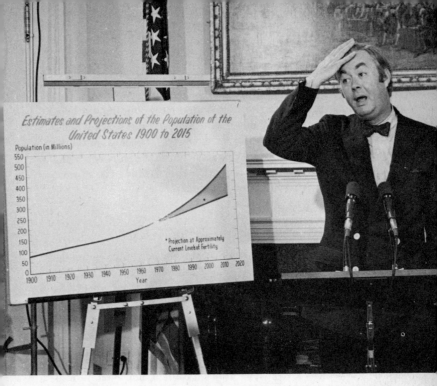

Estimates and Projections of the Population of the United States 1900 to 2015

his associates, Vice President Spiro T. Agnew (". . . you've seen one city slum, you've seen them all"). Agnew, who considers himself President Nixon's "personal representative" for America's cities, made Moynihan's very same point before taking office. "All too often," he said, "participation of the poor has been construed to mean playing both doctor and patient. . . . But let us not confuse disclosure of symptoms as a substitute for the wisdom of trained professionals."[39] "You don't learn from people suffering from poverty," said Agnew at another point, "but from experts who have studied the problem."[40]

For his part, "Doctor" Moynihan might just have considered for a moment that the Poor People's March on Washington, which happened a year before the Poverty Program was declared, as well as the incredible organizing in the South—the sit-ins that predated this program by four years—were somehow "symptomatic" that at least one seg-

205

ment of the poor knew what was happening to them. But even more important, he might also have "diagnosed" the sickness of those who don't rebel, of the white and black poor who, enduring a life of poverty, reflect a perverse political and economic system, a system that can repress and alienate people to the point where they believe the normal channels of politics simply don't work.

THE DOCTOR'S MEDICINE

In early 1970 Moynihan sent Nixon his now famous memo suggesting a government attitude of "benign neglect" of black people. Black people were obviously upset about the memo; but considering the doctor's "prescriptions" for poverty, they might have been thankful for such neglect. Summing up his vision for the next generation of poor blacks, in an earlier memo to President-elect Nixon, Moynihan said:

> They are not going to become capitalists, nor even middle-class functionaries. But it is fully reasonable to conceive of them being transformed into a stable working-class population: truck drivers, mail carriers, assembly-line workers—people with dignity, purpose, and in the United States a very good standard of living indeed.[41]

An elaboration of Moynihan's concept of "dignity" and "purpose" was to be revealed in his later role as chief architect of Nixon's welfare bill. With some rather obvious immodesty, Moynihan called the bill, which would give a family of four a maximum of $1600 a year, "the most important piece of social legislation in 35 years—one of the dozen or half-dozen most important bills in American history. . . . "[42]

The legislation's allowance—$33 per person per month—is actually lower than that already provided by every state but seven and in total would benefit only seven percent more welfare recipients.[43] At the same time the bill would require that people on welfare travel anywhere in the country where a job was available. Asked if the bill's work incentive provisions wouldn't force people into jobs that weren't meaningful, Moynihan exploded. "Middle class aesthetes are going around saying what is meaningful, what is meaningful employment," he said. "Most people work for a living to earn money for themselves and their families. They don't ask whether what they are doing is meaningful."[44]

Yet if all this weren't enough to be thankful for, Moynihan's "benign neglect," poor black (and white) people might consider another of his earlier "prescriptions." Back in 1966, as Lyndon B. Johnson was sending thousands of young men to an early death in Vietnam, Moynihan was suggesting that the armed forces be used as a way of "socializing" the poor.

> I would hold that a whole generation of poor Negroes and whites are missing their chance to get in touch with American society. Once they pass through and beyond the selective service screen they are very near gone for good in terms of the opportunity to become genuinely functioning, self-sufficient individuals. Civil rights as an issue is fading. The poverty program is headed for dismemberment and decline. Expectations of what can be done in America are receding. *Very possibly our best hope is seriously to use the armed forces as a socializing experience for the poor— particularly the Southern poor—until somehow their environment begins turning out equal citizens.*[45] (author's italics)

Moynihan's use of the Army to "socialize" the poor is a startling example of some grotesque ideological values entwined in the language of professionalism. What kind of science do you use to arrive at such conclusions? What does socializing mean? Do you socialize people by teaching them how to take orders? What laboratory experiments free from subjective values could possibly have been made? For urban doctors there are supposedly no political questions, such as

207

who gets what and through what process. When you are dealing with "medicine" and "science" rather than "politics," those who are trained as doctors make the diagnosis and prescribe the cure.

Moynihan's brand of science mongering can also be used by "doctors" who have converted their field of practice. After former Boston mayor John F. Collins became a Visiting Professor of Urban Affairs at MIT (with funds from the Ford Foundation grant Moynihan had defended against giving to the people with the "cancer"), he was quick to see the possibilities of masking political judgments under the banner of science. "The citizens of America," said Collins, "have finally realized that the business of running our cities cannot properly be left to the random operation of the political process."[46]

One might imagine that Mayor Collins preferred to see his own election to office as something more than the random operation of the political process. But as a professor, one must deal in the currency at hand—objectivity and science. According to Collins, who is also a partner in Urban Systems, Incorporated, a private firm specializing in advice to government agencies (it includes other MIT and Harvard faculty in addition to the president of Cabot, Cabot, and Forbes, a large real-estate-development firm), we must get rid of such approaches as intuition, guesswork, argument, debate, and consultation, the only kinds of tools we once had available.[47] Now, in five minutes of computer time, says Collins, we can see how an urban policy will work. "Intuition and humanitarian impulses when dealing with complex areas such as a city," complained the former mayor, "can only be relied upon to produce the wrong answer far more often than not."[48]

At another point, Collins made clear who was to be marshaled to write the computer programs. "Now we must find a workable, profit-oriented mechanism," he exhorted, "by which the great talents of systems-oriented industry can be brought to bear on the needs of society."* Following the well-worn path of government subsidies for the corporations, Collins outlines a vast new centralized enterprise, similar to those described earlier (see pages 86–90) setting about to solve our problems:

> I visualize the creation of a public-private corporate entity, with policy representation including the federal government, the nation's mayors, the nation's governors, and the private sector. Into this organization can be channeled funds from the public sector and the private sector, to be used by the corporation in a joint effort to identify the tasks, to reorder the priorities, and to develop plans to which the private sector can bring its systems analysis, mission-oriented problem solving potential. Think, if you will, of the number of customers that such an enterprise would have if it were able to look back at 12 months of research and advertise a new systems-oriented way to dispose of refuse. Imagine that in addition it could offer to do any one of a dozen things in the litany of unmet urban needs, while perhaps through a licensing arrangement create a revolving fund and so make possible honorable profit and improvement of our urban environment simultaneously.[49]

Thus, as this centralized, public-private "corporate entity," with full representation by the urban-industrial complex, marshaling their scientific tools of systems analysis,† sets about to "reorder the priorities," the people are once again left as spectators. Those whose priorities are being shuffled by this elite group of government officials, industry leaders, and their experts, are supposed to sit back, in the

---

* In this view, incidentally, he seems to be in concert with Lawrence Lessing, a writer for *Fortune* magazine. According to Lessing, "The major problem . . . is to find some profit-oriented mechanism by which the great talents of systems-oriented industry can be brought to bear on the great needs of the cities." (*Fortune*, January 1968, p. 221.)

† "Systems" and "systems analysis" refer to mathematical techniques for viewing many consequences of a particular action. They were developed during World War II to examine alternative military strategies.

hope that the right formula will be devised—perhaps tax write-downs, depreciation allowances, or outright subsidy— that will in effect use the people's taxes to put "honorable" profit in the coffers of industry. The patient, to borrow the Agnew–Moynihan analogy, is diagnosed, and the doctors' cure must fit not only him but the corporations as well. At least the medical patient has an easier time changing his doctor.

VII
Toward Liberation

AT THE VERY BEGINNING of this book, I described my involvement in advocacy planning, a form of city planning and architectural practice where professionals plead the cause of the poor and the disenfranchised before government forums. In my view and that of many others who were considered "radical" planners at the time, these actions would help make a reality of the democratic vision of power shared by all the interest groups. In a highly technical society, we argued, the availability of technical help to all groups was a critical requisite for true power sharing. The use of their own experts in planning and architecture was going to give the poor a strong voice at the places where decisions about their lives were being made.

Indeed, we were able to delay or make changes in some urban-renewal and highway plans. But we were to learn the limited extent of our influence. It took me some effort, including writing this book, to understand that we would be restricted to manipulating the pieces of welfare programs, born in the rhetoric of human compassion, yet whose ultimate result was to strengthen the hand of those who already determined the social existence of the poor. Contrary to popular mythology, planning did not bring socialism—in fact, it became a sophisticated weapon to maintain the exist-

ing control under a mask of rationality, efficiency, and science.

Advocacy planning and other citizen-participation programs could help maintain this mask by allowing the poor to administer their own state of dependency. The poor could direct their own welfare programs, have their own lawyers, their own planners and architects, so long as the economic structure remained intact—so long as the basic distribution of wealth, and hence real power, remained constant.

Resource commitments, such as $50 billion to an inter-

state highway system, for example, are made at forums like
the Clay Commission, where the interests of the highway
industries are represented (see Chapter III, pp. 69–78). We
could play at the game of citizen participation so long as
participation was limited to amelioration. We might be able
to depress some highways rather than have elevated structures; we might be able to shift the location of some highway routes; and we might even be able to get better relocation payments for those displaced. But we could not change
the program from one of building highways to redistribut-
ing the wealth of the highway corporations to the disenfranchised so that they could decide on their own programs,
be they building housing, schools, hospitals, or indeed highways.

By looking at the alliance that has developed between
politicians, planners and industry, it should now be clear
that both liberal and conservative reforms within the existing structure of American society cannot change the inequi-
ties of that society. Grafting a system of pluralist mechanisms, like advocacy planning, to this structure cannot solve
the dilemma of the basically undemocratic nature of societies which are based on a capitalist model. The problem of
trying to promote democracy in a capitalist economy through
such mechanisms is that those with more economic means
simply have more ability to control their personal and
political lives.* In terms of city-planning realities, those who

* On this point, I would have few arguments with some conservatives. According to William F. Buckley, Jr., conservative writer, editor, TV personality
and former candidate for Mayor of New York City:

It is a part of the conservative intuition that economic freedom is the most
precious temporal freedom, for the reason that *it alone* gives to each one
of us, in our comings and goings in our complex society, sovereignty—and
over that part of existence in which by far the most choices have in fact
to be made, and in which it is possible to make choices, involving oneself,
without damage to other people. And for the further reason that without
economic freedom, political and other freedoms are likely to be taken
from us. (Buckley, William F., Jr., *Up from Liberalism*, Bantam Books
[paperback], New York, 1968, p. 156.)

I concur with this, except of course where Mr. Buckley says it is possible

213

already have economic power control the distribution of political power. Corporations can use their financial leverage to influence politicians who in turn pass legislation to build highways, pay for urban renewal and self-serving job-training programs. As a result, corporations sell more autos, more oil, more asphalt, increase their real-estate holdings (while increasing their tax depreciation on these holdings) and train their work force. This in turn increases their financial power, which gives them still more political leverage.

In trying to achieve a pluralist society through advocacy planning there is an attempt to balance off the interests of those with financial power, who can buy planning expertise and the material goods they want, such as better housing and better schools, against those who can only ask what they want. If those who already control the economy and the government were *willing* to share power, then of course the problem would be one of *articulating* and arguing the needs of different interest groups.

But within the present economic structure of our society, simply giving the poor more access to planning expertise doesn't basically change their chances of getting the same goods and services as wealthier citizens. What it gives them is more power to compete among themselves for the government's welfare products. These are products designed by both liberals and conservatives who promote or at least accept welfare as some combination of paternalistic gestures —getting the poor to be more "productive," "self-respecting" citizens with "dignity" and "purpose," or, more basically, just plain protection money to make sure the status quo will not be disrupted. The leaders of industry allow urban "doctors" like Moynihan and Logue to generate programs so long as they require the minimum amount of funds necessary to

to make economic choices for oneself without damage to other people. Surely he understands laissez-faire economics well enough to know that as some win in the competitive game of exercising individual economic freedoms, others lose.

214

Demonstration at a meeting on New York City's "Master Plan"

pacify the poor and especially if large amounts of money can be channeled directly toward business to induce it to solve the urban crisis through programs like urban renewal, highways and "law and order."

Pluralist opportunities are therefore a necessary, but hardly sufficient, condition for real social equality. For such equality to occur, pluralism must be tied to a political ideology which deals directly with the means of equally distributing economic power.

A JUST OUTPUT

Having argued the case against American capitalism, I have not meant to imply that we should embrace an equally repressive socialist economic system. The Soviet Union is controlled by centralized bureaucratic institutions as unresponsive as those of the United States. Socialism, which I

215

define simply as the equal sharing of all resources of a society by all its people, is not an end in itself. Socialist man would hardly be better off than capitalist man if the society's attitudes were still repressive ones. Any form of politics will ultimately fail if it is not consistent with people's most fundamental needs for cooperation and a sense of love and joy in human experience—in essence, a humane existence. Socialism does not create this condition; rather, it allows it to occur—it *lets the society be humane.* In capitalist society, people can, of course, be humane and non-competitive, but only *in spite of* a system that gives every incentive to do otherwise.

But the problem of relying on any centrally controlled economic system, be it capitalist or socialist, as the sole precondition for humane cultural values can be seen by looking at the results of planning in the United States and Russia. Planning in both countries (more explicitly stated in Russia) is rationalized on the basis of making production efficient through centralized or "comprehensive" control. Drawing on the lessons of duplication and inefficiency caused by competitive battles of individual private entrepreneurs, planners proposed that by elimination of conflict and rationalization of production, all consumers would ultimately benefit by paying lower prices for their products. While the United States does not engage in formal five-year plans, the kind of informal planning engaged in by a military or urban-industrial complex is in fact a form of central planning and control for allocating the country's productive resources.

The danger of planning under both of these economic systems is the loss of personal control—planning can make sense to us only when the product being produced at the lower price grows from our needs, not from the norms of those in power. Planning may make it cheaper to produce war products, or more highways, but if we want to stop making these things, the concept of "efficient production" means little to us—in fact, its very efficiency makes it all the more impervious to our intervention. Viewing production this way, we can no longer aim simply at creating an efficient output—more importantly, we must aim at creating a cultural existence, a way of life, which requires *just outputs*. For example, if a community decides that a better architectural environment or a better educational program is to be produced, its way of measuring the usefulness of these programs would not result from calculating how much more money will be made through "keeping the workers happy" or by giving them more skills, but rather from evaluating the effects of a better architectural environment and better forms of education on the quality of people's lives.

For an economic system of socialism to support a humane cultural existence, it would have to operate at a level of social organization at which our involvement in determining the just outputs would be more immediate than is now possible. To do this, we must be able to control the economic means of satisfying needs where these needs themselves are most immediately felt—at the level of small groups of people, a neighborhood, or a small city rather than at higher levels of state or national government. Rarely do we in our daily lives sense a need for nationwide decision-making, except, of course, when such a need is imposed on us by national and corporate leaders, as for example in the case of the Indochina War. We rarely feel the need for nationwide or statewide programs in education, except again when this need is imposed on us by a government apparatus which happens to exist and distributes money on state or national levels of organization.

A system of community socialism (as opposed to either private enterprise or centralized socialism), in which the economic institutions would grow from the smaller governing units in the society, is a model which would allow social outputs to be determined by the people most immediately affected by them. The size of the governing unit, be it called a commune, a neighborhood or a city, would be determined

217

by arrival at a balance between the size necessary to produce certain products economically and the size at which people have an ability to actively participate in governing themselves.*

Community socialism could create the conditions which would allow our society to go beyond our present mock-egalitarian planning programs. The mixture of low-, middle-, and upper-income families, for example, that many of today's "progressive" planners see as a way of giving a neighborhood "vitality" and "getting people to understand each other," no matter how successful, still reflects the basic competitive nature of capitalism; some must win and some must lose. Under the planners' mixed-neighborhood program, the losers and winners are allowed to rub shoulders with each other—middle-class parents can give their children a chance to see what "life is really like."

The point here is not that "all kinds of people" shouldn't be able to live together. Rather, the makeup of a neighborhood, commune, or whatever it's called should ultimately be based on the free choice of individuals coming together to create a common way to live, not simply because planners are trying to create neighborhoods with bourgeois "vitality." It's only when people have the equal financial means, which community socialism in turn can provide, that people can form groupings on an equal basis and create a mutually arrived-at existence.

Of course, even under community socialism, many decisions and programs go beyond local boundaries; interde-

---

* Two American historians, William Appleman Williams and Gar Alperovitz, have called for decentralized socialist economic systems. Though he would begin with the assumption that technology has allowed this form of government by permitting a great amount of decentralization, Alperovitz notes, "In cases where this was false (transportation, heavy industry, perhaps power) the large confederate unit of the region or integrated unit of the nation-state would be appropriate." In "The Possibility of Decentralized Democratic Socialism in America" (unpublished mimeograph), The Cambridge Institute, Cambridge, Massachusetts. See also Williams, William Appleman, "An American Socialist Community?," *Liberation*, June 1969.

218

pendencies between regions and communities will naturally require some degree of centralization. The most obvious would involve pollution control, transportation, and the allocation of natural resources. Yet programs which may at first seem a natural case for centralization, such as a national highway system, may still be determined in large part by local interests. To arrive at a balance between local and central control, one would have to examine, in each case, the repressive effects of "central-tending" organizational forms.

It might be economically efficient, for example, to plan a nationwide or regional highway system without having to consider a local neighborhood's opposition to its construction; longer distances and more expensive construction or not building some roads at all may be involved. Yet in spite of this, it should still be possible for people to decide that it's more important for them to have a small-scale democratic governing unit than to provide the most efficient transportation system. The same can be seen in designing hospitals or schools. Large hospitals or large schools may reduce the direct cost of treating patients or educating students. In this case the depersonalized environments for healing, learning and human contact that these places have usually produced would have to be measured against the economic efficiency created by centralizing schools or hospitals.

A few years ago, for example, I talked to a group of public-housing residents about what they liked and disliked in their project. The only point people could agree on was that they liked a clinic that had been built by remodeling and interconnecting a few of the apartments. Bedrooms became examining rooms and living rooms were turned into reception areas. The people said they liked the "warm," "friendly" atmosphere compared to the large city hospital to which they had to go before the clinic was built. When I asked the clinic director what he thought about the place, he said it was working well but that they were thinking of replacing it with a new, larger building. If they were taking care of

219

20,000 families, he said, instead of the 5,000 that lived in the project, they could make much more economical use of a blood-testing machine.

Obviously a clinic needs to test blood, but it's not so obvious that doing this economically (which presumably means that more blood tests can be made) necessarily means a better situation to live in, nor, I might add, does it necessarily mean that a larger number of people will even have better health care. In all probability, many poor people use the dehumanized welfare health facilities only when they find themselves in extreme predicaments. With more comfortable health facilities available, they would probably tend to use them before they found themselves in critical health.

While groupings of socialist governments can form the base of an egalitarian and humane society, this form will not of itself lead to the revolution in people's attitudes and values necessary to sustain such a society. It will not of itself make people more sensitive in dealing with themselves and others (it will not, for example, end racism and sexism), it will not make people more sensitive to ecological needs, nor will it make them more sensitive to their architectural needs. For such a sensitivity to occur will require a kind of cultural change in which people see the establishment of a governing form like community socialism not as an instrument of achieving a competitive economic advantage over other economic forms, but as an instrument to support a fundamentally new culture.

We cannot wait for a humane form of socialism to miraculously arise and establish such a culture—for a revolution which does not itself feed on more humane values will ultimately duplicate the present repression with a more rational economic system. To be for socialism and against capitalism as a more efficient way of delivering consumer goods is an attitude based on the values of a culture which sees expediency and efficiency as the boundaries of progress. Our problem is not simply to destroy capitalism, but to do this through the creation of a culture which will not tolerate the repressive and competitive values which capitalism has already induced us to accept. In this new culture, community socialism is simply one norm (the governing system already existing in embryonic stages in cooperatives and communes) in an expanding set of possibilities for both peaceful and militant action. Planning and architecture present an important opportunity for strengthening this process.

THE NEW PROFESSIONAL

Having rejected the traditional role of advocate planner within the present structure of government does not mean rejecting the expert's role in creating the liberated society. For the planner, environment-making would be used to move toward more humane attitudes by presenting ways of designing and using architecture as an alternative to the present oppressive ways for doing this. As environmental professionals, we can begin this process by realizing that our present solutions, our ways of going about planning and designing, have been conditioned in good part by the need to continue our existence as a restricted professional group. Our economic existence and our power relation to other people has depended on this group identity. We can introduce new ideas, even radical ideas, into this guild—so long as these ideas can be marketed or managed by this group. We can move beyond this form of elitism by structuring our existence in relation to our social community's needs rather than our professional community's needs. Instead of remaining the "outside expert" trying to resolve the conflicting needs of the low-middle-high-income metropolis, or simply "helping the poor," we can become participants in our own community's search for new family structures or other changing patterns of association, and participants in the process of creating physical settings which would foster these ways of life—in effect, we become a part of, rather

221

than an expert for, cultural change. A step in this process is to explore and make our community aware of the causes of environmental oppression—the nature of how real-estate speculation affects design, for example—and to promote the creation of alternative environmental forms.

Design opportunities can be used as a way of explaining the advantages of community ownership and management of all income-producing ventures—the factories, the housing and the shopping places. The design of housing in particular could expose people to the possibilities of designing for themselves, and to more communal patterns of living together. A communal building, where people share facilities and spaces, would present an alternative to the present single-family house or apartment "unit"—an environmental condition based on the duplication of facilities which in turn induces maximum consumption. The communal or shared environment embodies a cultural change inherently antagonistic to the capitalist tendency to expand consumer markets.

Designing innovative educational places as alternatives to "the school" is another possible way of moving toward a better future society through action now. As a case in point, two years ago my architecture students at MIT and I were involved in helping a group of middle-class white suburbia teenagers trying to design their own learning place, "a liberated zone" as they called it. The liberated zone was to be a place where high-school students could come together outside their home and school situation in a personal environment for finding out about themselves and what they wanted their education to be like. While this place has yet to be built, it raised some new possibilities for design processes that explore new cultural attitudes. By posing specific design solutions as alternatives to the present repression, the design process gave people a chance to understand their present feelings by projecting or acting out an environmental existence. It required that people think about how their

222

The existing high school

present attitudes were conditioned by existing cultural attitudes. In one session, for example, I asked what impression they'd like this "liberated zone" to have on someone driving past it on his way home from work.

> We should make it Colonial on the outside and do what we want inside. That way people driving by will not get upset about it.

> What do you mean Colonial on the outside—we'll make it the way we want all over. Let's not worry about what other people think.

They also thought about how adults might react—as some felt, parents had the power to close the place. Some students saw the building as a display of their ideas, like a badge worn on their sleeve.

223

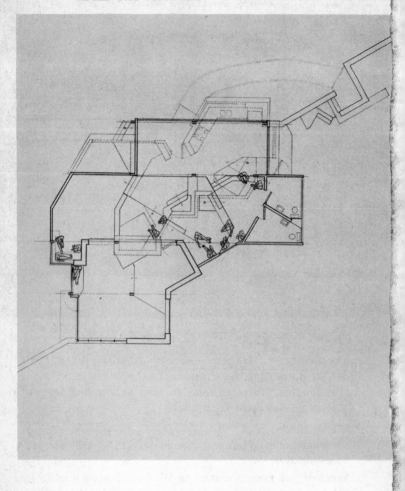

The Liberated Zone: alternative designs directed by William Holland (above) and Joan Fleischnick (opposite)

224

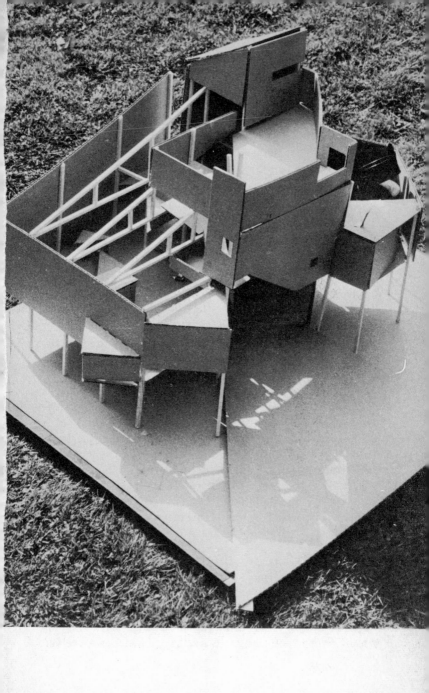

I don't think my parents will like it. Right now I'm home after school, and my parents like that. If the center gets built, I'll go there after school, be home for supper, and go there again at night. They're not going to like that.

How can they solve that problem—the fact is, you are isolating them.

I don't know—maybe have another baby.

Is this place just for kids? What about adults? Can they come?

Adults can come, but on our terms. They can't come in like they usually do, judging us as adults, giving us a lot of bullshit about how they're going to close the place down if they don't like it. They can come in and argue, but they have to do it on the basis of equals. We can argue but they can't pull rank on us.

In one sense even the failure to be able to build the project is also one of its successes. Having described a more humane environmental existence, having tasted possibilities which the present institutions cannot accept for fear of losing their own domination, the contrast between the present and a possible better future becomes even more apparent. In the cases where students attempted to acquire funds or land it wasn't available; instead, the town offered them the basement of a town office building—where they could remain under the watchful eyes of the authorities. The students' "liberated zone" design was in effect a demand on the existing structure of domination. Having to confront the kind of reality that rejects a demand for a more humane educational existence makes students aware of the need for more radical changes.

Raising demands around the needs of humane existence rather than those that our present system can deliver approximates the kinds of "non-reformist reforms" that the radical French economist André Gorz has proposed as a workers' strategy for attaining a socialist society.[1] This type of reform, according to Gorz, "is one which is conceived

226

not in terms of what is possible within the framework of a given system and administration, but in view of what should be made possible in terms of human needs and demands." He differentiates this kind of revolutionary reform from the "reformist reform," which he defines as "one which subordinates its objectives to the criteria of rationality and practicability of a given system and policy. Reformism rejects those objectives and demands—however deep the need for them—which are incompatible with the preservation of the system."[2] As an illustration of how non-reformist reforms are to be determined, Gorz notes:

> Is it reformist, for example, to demand the construction of 500,000 new housing units a year, or a real democratization of secondary and higher education? It is impossible to know beforehand. One would have to decide first whether the proposed housing program would mean the expropriation of those who own the required land, and whether the construction would be a socialized public service, thus destroying an important center of the accumulation of private capital; or if, on the contrary, this would mean subsidizing private enterprise with taxpayers' money to guarantee its profits.
>
> One must also know whether the intention is to build workers' housing anywhere that land and materials can be cheaply bought, or if it is to construct lodgings as well as new industry according to optimum human and social criteria.[3]

GUERRILLA ARCHITECTURE

The nature of environmental demands made on the established order can be at the scale of 500,000 housing units Gorz refers to or on the scale of one housing unit; the critical element is both the nature of the demand and how people raise the demand—the style of action. In this way the questions to which a planning move must submit are: Does it help promote political consciousness of the people? Does the demand expose the repression of the established order? Does it address itself to the people's real needs? And are there ways that people can act on these demands with some hope of success? And will successes and even failures lead to the kind of political consciousness which in turn leads to further political acts and the creation of a larger movement for change?

In what might be called guerrilla architecture, I've found that the style of action, in fact, plays a crucial role in determining the effectiveness of a demand. This is more clearly the case with squatters' housing in South America[4] and also increasingly so in the United States. In Boston a group of low-income families recently squatted in newly renovated apartments in their neighborhood just before the higher-income tenants were scheduled to move in. Within a month the landlord was forced to lower his rents and the public-housing agency to provide a rent subsidy for the families. In

We need good
low-cost housing.
We will take
what is ours.

Necisitamos buen
viendas baratas.
Tomemos lo
que es nuestro.

SUPPORT THE SQUATTERS
APOYEN LOS SQUATTERS

New York City similar actions have forced city agencies to make housing available for low-income people. In one case the squatters organized under the banner of "Operation Move-In." Working at night, with crowbars, the people opened doors and windows of apartments scheduled for demolition by the city. The apartments were often in reasonably good condition. (At one point the city had maintenance crews deliberately destroy toilet fixtures in buildings to deter the squatters—but later conceded to the opposition.)

It's true that many of the people in these apartments still face eviction by the authorities. But this is a factor which must be measured against the alternate of planning and waiting for housing that will probably not happen at all. Another factor is how this direct action counters the usual feeling of hopelessness in poor neighborhoods. "The ones who were willing to do it were pretty strong people," said one of the squatter organizers. "When they first went in it was like they were liberated—they were exhilarated." After the initial forces of the operation more and more people signed up on waiting lists for new squatter actions.[5] The

229

larger this group becomes, the more difficult it will be for the city to actually remove people without providing alternate housing. It becomes a process by which the disenfranchised become aware of their potential power when they are willing to act together.

People's Park at Berkeley, California, where local people took over a parking lot owned by the University of California and designed and built a park, is another case for guerrilla architecture. "A long time ago," said the original position paper on the park, "the Costanoan Indians lived in the area now called Berkeley. They had no concept of land ownership. They believed that land was under the care and guardianship of the people who used it and lived on it." The paper described how the land was taken from the Indians by Catholic missionaries, from the missionaries by the Mexican government, from that government by the American government and then sold to American settlers, who in turn sold

it to real-estate developers, who finally sold it to the University of California. "When the university comes with its land title," concludes the paper, "we will tell them: 'Your land title is covered with blood. We won't touch it. You people ripped off the land from the Indians a long time ago. If you want it back now, you will have to fight for it again.' "[6]

As the university decided to call in the civil authorities, they did indeed have to fight. The police and national guard retook the park—but not without people throughout the world becoming aware of the repression which can be unleashed in the name of protecting private property. People's Park is now a fenced-in lot where you pay to park your car (not many people use it). As a form of guerrilla architecture it served to advance the cause of liberation by making

231

people aware of the hostile forces they face in bringing about change—even with a benign project like a park and in dealing with what is supposedly a humanitarian institution like a university.

In my own experience with guerrilla architecture, I've also seen the efficacy of using direct action rather than adapting to existing bureaucratic techniques. In one case, working with volunteer neighborhood organizations and MIT architecture students, I helped design and build a squatter community on a Boston parking lot. At another time, again with architecture students, I helped design and build a bus shelter at MIT—the actual building was fabricated earlier and then dropped on the site in a few minutes. The point of both these projects which were organized around very different needs, was to use direct action to force the established institutions and their procedures to change. It was a strategy of getting something done, but in a political context that demonstrated the usefulness of direct action as opposed to making paper demands which could easily be delayed or rejected.

In the case of the MIT bus shelter, students and staff were watching multimillion-dollar buildings sprouting up all over the campus to accommodate "vital" research and education functions, such as a new space research center, while their mundane problems, like waiting for a bus in the New England climate, were unanswered. The situation was a microcosm of where the university's priorities were.

The design of the bus shelter was to include everything we thought might make it pleasant for people as they waited for a bus. It had a free coffee machine, a heater, a free telephone and flowers. None of the machines worked and the flowers were plastic. The situation wasn't real (it was a mock bus shelter, after all). The point was to exaggerate the unreality in order to dramatize the need for a real bus shelter. The shelter was opened with great pomp: TV interviews with students who built the shelter and a ribbon-cutting ceremony that featured a bus driver who left his bus to cut the ribbon. Probably some combination of favorable response of people to the shelter and the embarrassment of having a piece of "junk" messing up the "beautiful" campus entrance moved the university to action: several months later they put up their own shelter. The approach was a bit different. There was no coffee, no heater, no telephone, no flowers, and the director of the transit system made a speech.

The squatter project centered on traditional urban-renewal projects in the black and Puerto Rican section of Boston. It was an area that urban-renewal chief Edward J. Logue had supposedly been "planning with people"; only as it had often turned out in the past, he'd been planning with a certain kind of people, homeowners and private developers. The tenants, the rooming-house people were to be "relocated." Many were told they'd be relocated in the same area, but it never happened. As more and more buildings were demolished or remodeled by middle-class people taking advantage of cheap in-town locations, more and more of the lowest income people were being forced out. Finally, a group of militant neighborhood organizations decided to stop this process. On a parking lot in the urban-renewal area where several buildings had recently been torn down, the people sat in and kept cars from parking. The police arrested the demonstrators, but the next day they came back and camped on the parking-lot land. Within a few hours after daybreak the squatter community of about one hundred people began to take shape. By the time police arrived, the people, working with architecture students, had their buildings established on the land—"Tent City" was proclaimed as fact. The police decided not to invade the "city," which by this time began to attract more and more people from the neighborhood.

At first we built housing, but as more people began to come, more ideas came with them. Some people built a city hall; others built a medical center and then came an interdenominational religious structure. Shelters took shape from anything that was available—discarded crates, old signs and tents. The place was always alive with barbecues, bongo drums, speeches and discussion groups. At times the music and talk would end abruptly as one of the community leaders would announce the result of the latest negotiations with the city officials.

Occupancy of the parking lot lasted four days before the neighborhood groups were forced to leave. But by that time they'd won promises from the city which eventually stopped much of the relocation (until new housing was available in their own neighborhood). It also led to the election of a neighborhood committee to oversee the urban-renewal plan (the first time in this country that such a committee was ever elected) and an agreement to turn over many city-owned and slumlord-owned buildings to low-income neighborhood groups. Working with one of these organizations,

Tent City, Boston

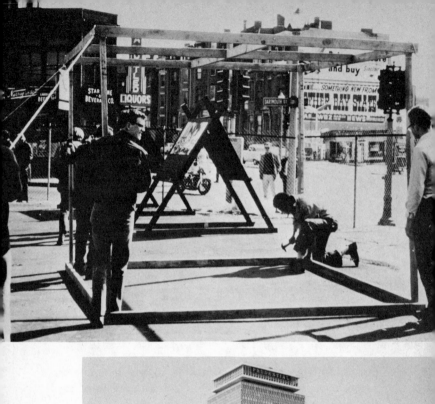

my students and I have been able to redesign and then reconstruct several of these buildings for a number of neighborhood families.

The style and scale of such a guerrilla design process obviously won't come near to meeting the quantity of environmental needs in this country; there would have to be more radical change in most of our institutions for this to happen. Its usefulness, however, is as a strategic tactic in an ongoing struggle for change. It sometimes makes possible short-term success while often publicly exposing the need for sweeping changes in housing policies. It illustrates that the only way the environmental needs of the disenfranchised will be met in our present society is through the process of struggle. And it is a process not easily co-opted by the existing institutions. Since these institutions are based on the concept of private property, they must radically alter their own structure for domination in order to meet the squatters' demands.

236

The present style of most advocacy planning, on the other hand, induces people to accept the bureaucratic norms of the present social institutions. In order to deal with the official bureaucracy, the neighborhood group will create one of its own. People attend public meetings and present in the form of maps and written reports requests for new plans or changes in official ones. These meetings are time-consuming, often dull forums for people to "let off steam." As time drags on and nothing happens, the community's energies are diffused and its criticism is blunted. The process becomes a classic form of manipulating the opposition into submission.

With a form of direct action like guerrilla architecture, the authorities must deal with what is already built. It is they who are put in a defensive position—they, the authori-

Neighborhood people and architecture students rehabilitate abandoned building in Boston

ties, have the choice of either letting the people stay in facilities that are obviously needed (as in the case of the squatters) or exposing the oppressive nature of their control to more people through the publicity of the removal process (as in the case of squatters and the People's Park). The people either win their demands or at least expose the oppression of those who control the environment. At the very least they don't waste their time in a ritual of participation which they can't control.

Guerrilla architecture also moves in the direction of cultural change by beginning to break the traditional bond between people and professionals in the creation of an architectural environment. While professionals were used in some of the cases I described, the unique quality of this form of architecture is that it depends less on professionals for its success—popular participation in environmental decisions begins to emerge.

ENVIRONMENT AS CULTURAL REVOLUTION

Realizing that our present theories have been molded by the perverse cultural context in which they now thrive, we must be especially careful not to use new, more open cultural attitudes as a pretext for delivering the old design approaches. It would be absurd, for example, to apply the concepts of hierarchical form described in Chapter IV to more humane, more immediately felt, small-scale communities. The very notion of an environmental hierarchy, with more or less "important-looking" symbolic buildings, is a device to awe the people who use the state's or the corporation's environment. This approach would be a contradiction in the process of liberation since it has no roots in the way people use an environment as they themselves define it.

The problem, then, is not how to bring planners "closer to the people," as one familiar argument goes, but how to create the kind of cultural change where people are free of a dependency on such experts. This means creating design situations where people no longer feel compelled to emulate the aesthetic values of the latest architectural tastemakers, but are free to explore their own environmental needs. By making real decisions about their architecture, instead of being studied as subjects for social scientists to determine "involvement ratios," people could develop over time a new sensory awareness of how they are affected by the places they live in—and how in turn they can affect these places. By regenerating the design senses which have atrophied from their progressive lack of use over many generations, this process would in effect begin to develop the environmental dimension of a cultural revolution.

There is striking evidence in looking at what we tend to call primitive cultures that people are indeed capable of making more personally meaningful connections with their environment. In some of these societies, buildings aren't used simply as shelter against the weather. A potent example of how people have made an intimate match between their personal feelings and their environment can be seen in the Mbuti pygmy tribes in the Congo's Ituri Forest. The findings of Colin M. Turnbull, an English anthropologist, describing the pygmies' use of their environments contrast sharply with Western concepts of architecture. The pygmies, who survive by hunting, travel from place to place, setting up camps during their hunts. The location of their huts is closely tied to people's emotional attitude toward each other. If someone likes his neighbor, he'll face his entrance toward him; if not, he'll face his entrance in the opposite direction. If he already has an entrance and changes his feelings about a neighbor, he'll sew up the entrance and make another one. And if someone really dislikes his neighbor, he'll pick up his hut and move it to another part of the camp. According to Turnbull, ". . . the composition of each camp is ad hoc, responding to the needs of the moment

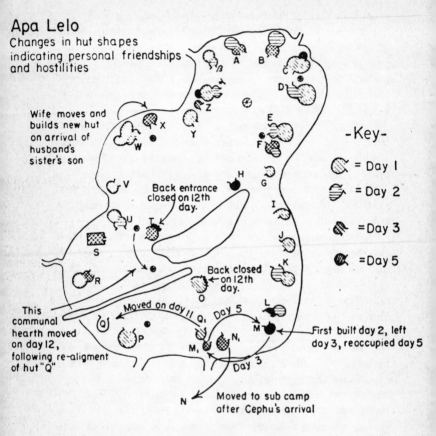

Apa Lelo
Changes in hut shapes indicating personal friendships and hostilities

Wife moves and builds new hut on arrival of husband's sister's son

Back entrance closed on 12th day.

Back closed on 12th day.

This communal hearth moved on day 12, following re-aligment of hut "Q"

Moved on day 11

Day 5

Day 3

First built day 2, left day 3, reoccupied day 5

Moved to sub camp after Cephu's arrival

-Key-

$\mathbb{C}$ = Day 1

$\mathbb{S}$ = Day 2

$\mathbb{N}$ = Day 3

$\mathbb{C}$ = Day 5

rather than any preconceived plan, or to any notion derived from tradition. The lines of division [the way the camp is broken into groupings] are never the same; the reasons for division are nearly always personal."[7]

The layout of the camp itself is directed toward relieving social tensions within the tribe. "Sites are even chosen," says Turnbull, "because they afford greater privacy between the various sections, thus minimizing any serious disputes that are in progress. Some interpersonal hostilities will persist, however, and it is these and not lineal [family] relationships that are reflected in the final fission, when the camp divides into a number of independent camps, or subbands, each going its own way."[8]

Of course it is very deceptive to carry any direct implications from one culture to another; that's not my purpose. What is useful, though, is to look seriously at radically different cultures, not to imitate them but to raise our level of awareness about a range of possibilities—it gives us a

Kano, Nigeria

proposition of what a liberated community might encompass. The pygmy community is an illustration of what could be called anti-monumental, anti-formalist acts of people creating their own environments. Examples such as medieval cities and towns, which resulted from the aggregate of many decisions over time, could also superficially describe the possible form qualities of longer-term communities.

Towns such as Kano, Nigeria, and some squatter settlements in Latin America, hardly an adequate model for what would be possible with the technology available in this country, again hint at form qualities of a more spontaneous, less bourgeois, "aesthetic" environment. In this architecture, complexity would not result in formal, preconceived aesthetic attitudes about "hierarchy," "jazz," "pop" or "variety," but a complexity where real differences in people's ways of living become apparent by real differences in their life spaces. Instead of buildings designed as visually pleas-

House designed, built, and lived in by Clarence Schmidt, Upstate N.Y.

Housing, New York

ing *objects* to be viewed and judged by professionals, this architecture would be an open-ended collective assembly of the many design decisions made by the people who actually use the environment.

But again, this attempt to describe and illustrate the qualities of an architecture which would grow from the experience of use rather than the norms of hierarchy, and monumentality, must itself be viewed as a way of generating possibilities, not defining outcomes. Not only would apparent cultural and historic differences contradict an adaptation of these forms, but, more importantly, the formal environment of a liberated society, by its very nature, growing from the experience of people creating their own environmental world, must necessarily await the opportunity for that experience to occur. That is, forms which grow from the experience of use (of living within these forms, adapting and changing them) should not rely heavily on pictorial qualities which are communicated and interpreted through "look at" experience.

243

AFTER THE PLANNERS

People housing themselves, Lima, Peru

WHAT ARE THEY GOING TO DO?

The obvious question now is that, given a radically new opportunity to shape their own places to live, won't people, especially poor and uneducated people, use the models of the architecture they already know? After all, they've been educated by the media and advertisements to value what business can make a profit at; even with their new freedom, won't they continue operating on the basis of their conditioned values?

These crucial questions occur again and again in attempting radical social change in a society where people have been induced to live in what Herbert Marcuse has called the "euphoria in unhappiness."[9] Freedom can hardly be used very freely when a person's mind and spirit have been warped by a system which limits the range of his choice in order to maintain itself. That is, you're hardly exercising a real choice by picking among a set of gimmicks promoted by business to make you *feel* you have a choice. Middle-class

245

Americans could be considered to have a choice, for example, in the sense that when they move to the suburbs they feel they have a choice between the Cape Cod colonial or the split-level ranch. But, in fact, they don't have the choice of living in radically different ways beyond the "unit" single-family house.

The early results of an approach where people design their own environments will probably not suit the needs of the people who have made the design; the experts will probably reject these efforts and call for more professional help. But as people use their own environments over time, they can be expected to know more about which designs are useful and which ones aren't. They won't need elaborate "user studies" to find out what's wrong since they, in contrast to the absentee expert, will, after all, be living in the environments they create.

The efficacy of even a crude form of popular architecture like squatter environments, for example, where expertise must be shared between the professional and the people, or, as more likely, completely taken over by the people, is that it begins to demystify the profession, destroying the former dependency relationship. People sense they can begin to act on their needs without waiting for the government or its experts to take care of them.

Yet does all this mean that everyone in the liberated society would have to become his own planner and architect? Not at all. More permanent environments than the examples I've described, especially in colder climates, would normally involve construction expertise beyond what most people could master. The crucial question here is not whether people can become technical experts in systems of buildings but whether or not people know enough about their own requirements for the use of architectural space to avoid being subservient to professionals. That is, people should be able to distinguish between the expert's personal judgments about architecture and his technical advice for making

246

environmental space come into being. Even in so-called technical decisions there are usually no clear distinctions between the expert's objective and subjective judgments. Certain technical solutions often result in people having more or less chances to alter their own living spaces. A decision to build a high-rise building, for example, involves much more complex and difficult construction techniques than a one- or two-story structure—a decision which in turn means that people are less able easily to alter their living space, such as adding another room when a new baby comes along. Yet that decision to construct living spaces in a tall building, rather than close to the ground, for example, may be the result of an architect's deciding that he needs a taller building to "balance" a "composition" of lower building forms.

To create a condition in which people can act on their own environmental needs, in which they can make the distinctions between the expert's technical and aesthetic judgments, requires a change in the consciousness of both the people and experts. It requires that people develop the willingness to design the form of their environment, to live in it, to adapt it to their needs. At the same time, the expert can accelerate this process by changing his traditional approach to architecture. Instead of an insistence on designing all buildings, as many architectural leaders have aimed at (a highly illusive goal which nevertheless influences our attitudes), we would begin to demystify the profession. We would show people how our closed professional guilds have helped alienate them from making decisions about their environments and we would attempt to transfer many of the useful skills we do have to them.

With its decentralized politics, a community-socialist organization would make the expert's actions more visible to those affected by what he does; its planning could then become defined by actual problems felt by the community. Elitist aesthetics like Venturi's pop architecture or Moynihan's ways of socializing the poor or Hall's "involvement ratios" would be more difficult to promote when they would have to be judged by the people actually affected rather than a cultural or technocratic elite. Furthermore, a socialist context which by its nature has no speculative builder as client changes the test of a solution's "rightness." It is no longer whether profits have been maximized but whether the people have been satisfied. Impulses to create new communal arrangements would be a free choice, unconditioned by whether the real-estate interests and banks can profit from such arrangements. If you really think there is a free environmental choice now, try getting a bank to lend you mortgage money for an unconventional building.

My emphasis on people's ability to make environmental decisions should not be confused with a vision of a pre-industrial, crafts-producing society with everybody building his own little house. While I and other architects find ourselves working at the level of handicrafts today (for lack of an appropriate technology to meet people's needs), that level of producing environment seems to me unnecessary and often undesirable. Constructing an environment through handicraft techniques can be a very personally satisfying way for a limited number of people to produce housing; I've seen this type of work in several country communes. But the opportunity we have today, given the unique industrial potential of this country and other industrial "giants," is the ability to produce the kind of building products which would make the manipulation of the environment more easily managed by large numbers of non-professionals. Thus far our technical capacity has helped produce the familiar blight that surrounds us—one perverse piece of minimum environment made to seem more acceptable by contrast to the next affront to our tolerance of adversity. This frustrating condition sometimes misleads us into denouncing the tools of industrial society while calling for those of a more humble time. But it is through many of these same tools, such as automation, that liberation from much of society's "shit work" can happen. A society intent on providing humane conditions for existence rather than the rhetoric of that intent could use its enormous productive capacity of industrialized products which would expand people's creative range for manipulating their environment.

Today the industrialization of housing in this country is moving rapidly toward the model of the mobile home. Already representing 25 percent of all new homes that are being produced, these minimum living packages give a grotesque hint of our future environment. But the problem with these homes is not that they are produced in factories; rather it is simply in the nature of the design—the fixed nature of the building shell, the ubiquitous finish of surfaces, and the lack of adaptability to design manipulation by the people who use them. A country which has the capacity to produce sophisticated instruments of mass destruction and containers carrying men to explore space, which must adapt to subtle variations in temperature, wind stress and the movement of the universe, should indeed have the ability to produce building products for humane living which are flexible enough to allow human changes in fixed positions here on earth.

To move this society to a sane use of its technology is a task of liberation obviously beyond the scope of any particular profession. It will take the accumulated consciousness of a multitude of us, acting on the belief that the end of our oppression must come from our everyday actions, from our refusal to participate in the insane destruction waged in our name, and from the change in cultural values we can promote through the work we know best. As people concerned about the creation of a better environment, we must see ourselves committed to a movement of radical political change which will be the condition for the existence of this environment.

It is no longer possible for us to masquerade as "disinterested," "objective" professionals, applying our techniques with equal ease to those clients we agree with as well as to those we disagree with. We are, in effect, the client for all our projects, for it is our own society we are affecting through our actions. By raising the possibilities of a humane way of producing places to live, by phasing out the elitist nature of environmental professionalism, we can move toward a time when we will no longer define ourselves by our profession, but by our freedom as people.

NOTES

INTRODUCTION

1. *Time*, September 12, 1969, p. 40.
2. "Chancellor Kiesinger Talks About Youth," *Look* magazine, November 12, 1966, p. 44.
3. Boston *Sunday Globe*, October 18, 1970, p. A-25.
4. Boston *Sunday Globe*, March 16, 1969, p. 18A.
5. *I. F. Stone's Bi-Weekly*, October 20, 1969, p. 1.

CHAPTER I

1. Webber, Melvin M., "Comprehensive Planning and Social Responsibility," American Institute of Planners *Journal*, November 1963, p. 241.
2. Davidoff, Paul, "Advocacy and Pluralism in Planning," American Institute of Planners *Journal*, November 1965.
3. Boston *Globe*, November 18, 1966.
4. Cited in Gans, Herbert J., "End Papers," *The Center Forum*, August 28, 1967, Vol. 2, No. 2. Published by the Center for Urban Education, a Regional Education Laboratory of the United States Office of Education, Department of Health, Education and Welfare.
5. See, for example, *The Federal Role in Urban Affairs*, hearings before the Subcommittee on Executive Reorganization of the Committee on Government Operations, U.S. Government Printing Office, Washington, D.C., 1966.
6. Ad placed by the Metropolitan College of Boston University in the Boston *Globe*, August 14, 1967, p. 7.
7. *Architectural and Engineering News*, June 1969, p. 8.
8. Schlesinger, Arthur M., Jr., "The Velocity of History," special essay in *Newsweek*, July 6, 1970, p. 32.
9. *Ibid.*, p. 34.
10. Association for Improving the Condition of the Poor (ACIP), Thirteenth Annual Report, 1856, p. 24. Cited in Lubove, Roy, *The Progressives and the Slums*, University of Pittsburgh Press, 1962, p. 7.
11. Veiller, Lawrence, *Housing Reform*, The Russell Sage

Foundation, New York, 1910, p. 5.

12. Address before the United States Conference of Mayors, Dallas, Texas, June 13, 1966. Published by the United States Department of Housing and Urban Development.

13. Morgenthau, Henry, *A National Constructive Programme for City Planning.*

Address, May 21, 1909. *Proceedings of the First National Conference on City Planning,* American Society of Planning Officials, 1967, pp. 59–60.

14. *The New York Times,* August 9, 1969, p. 10.

15. Lewis, Anthony, "A Talk with Warren on Crime, the Court, the Country," *The New York Times Magazine,* October 1969, p. 34.

CHAPTER II

1. In *I. F. Stone's Bi-Weekly,* Washington, D.C., April 15, 1968, p. 1.

2. Address given before the National Association of Manufacturers Congress of American Industry, New York, December 3, 1969, U.S. Department of Commerce news release, pp. 4, 14–15.

3. Todd, Richard, "George Wald: The Man, The Speech," *The New York Times Magazine,* August 17, 1969, p. 88.

4. *Business Week,* November 1, 1969, p. 67.

5. Martin, Richard, "Business Tackles the Ghetto," *The American Way,* May–June 1969, American Airlines publication, New York, p. 35.

6. Cohn, Jules, "Is Business Meeting the Challenge of Urban Affairs?," *Harvard Business Review,* March–April 1970.

7. *Ibid.*

8. Address by Robinson F. Parker, Chairman of the Board and Chief Executive Officer of Pittsburgh Plate Glass Industries, to National 1968 Industrial Conference Board, New York, January 10, 1968.

9. *Business Week,* December 6, 1969, pp. 145–46.

10. *Moody's Stock Survey,* November 10, 1969, Vol. 61, No. 45, p. 375.

11. *Ibid.,* p. 376.

12. *Ibid.,* p. 383.

13. Information on pollution agencies from *The New York Times,* December 7, 1970, pp. 1, 50.

14. Information on poverty agencies and consulting firms from *The New York Times,* November 8, 1970, pp. 1, 54, and *Hard Times,* October 13–20, 1969, No. 48, pp. 1, 2.

15. *The Wall Street Journal,* April 21, 1970, p. 1.

16. Ford, Henry II, *The Human Environment and Business,* Weybright and Talley, New York, 1970, p. 7.

17. *Ibid.,* p. 41.

18. *The New York Times,* November 9, 1969, p. 49.

19. *Ibid.*

20. Martin, *op. cit.,* p. 37.

21. Boston *Globe,* December 10, 1970, pp. 1, 14.

22. Cook, Ann, and Mack, Herbert, "Business in Education" in *Social Policy,* September–October 1970, pp. 4–11.

23. *Ibid.*, p. 11.
24. *Ibid.*, p. 8.
25. *Ibid.*, p. 9.
26. Burck, Gilbert, "A New Business for Business: Reclaiming Human Resources," *Fortune*, January 1968, pp. 161, 198.
27. Tornquist, Elizabeth, "Family Plan," *Hard Times*, October 6–13, 1969, p. 3.
28. *Ibid.*
29. Martin, *op. cit.*, p. 35.

30. Nadler, Leonard, "Helping the Hard-Core Adjust to the World of Work," *Harvard Business Review*, March–April 1970, pp. 117, 118.
31. Ad in *Harvard Business Review*, March–April 1970, p. 151.
32. Nadler, *op. cit.*, p. 123.
33. Burck, *op. cit.*, p. 202.
34. Ford II, *op. cit.*, pp. 39, 8, 51, 62.
35. Burck, *op. cit.*, p. 200.

CHAPTER III

1. Veiller, Lawrence, *Housing Reform*, The Russell Sage Foundation, New York, 1910, pp. 81–82.
2. Davies, Richard O., *Housing Reform During the Truman Administration*, University of Missouri Press, Columbia, Missouri, 1966, pp. 8–9. See also Abrams, Charles, *The Future of Housing*, Harper and Brothers, New York, London, 1946, pp. 210, 220. A good description of how New Deal housing programs were used by government to help industry appears in Bernstein, Barton J., "The New Deal: The Conservative Achievements of Liberal Reform," in Bernstein, Barton J., *Towards a New Past*, Vintage (paperback), New York, pp. 263–88.
3. Abrams, Charles, "Housing Policy—1937 to 1967," in Freiden, Bernard J., and Nash, William W., Jr., eds., *Shaping an Urban Future*, Massachusetts Institute of Technology Press, Cambridge, Mass., 1969, p. 37.

4. United States Federal Housing Administration, *FHA Underwriting Handbook*, 1938, Section 929.
5. *Ibid.*, Section 937.
6. Abrams, Charles, *Forbidden Neighbors*, Harper and Brothers, New York, 1955, p. 241.
7. *Ibid.*, p. 232.
8. Wallace, David A., "Beggars on Horseback," *Ends and Means of Urban Renewal*, Philadelphia Housing Association, Philadelphia, Pa., 1961, p. 47.
9. Abrams, Charles, "Homeless America, Part 2," in *The Nation*, December 28, 1946, Vol. 163, No. 26, p. 754.
10. Burchard, John, and Bush-Brown, Albert, *The Architecture of America: A Social and Cultural History*, Little, Brown & Company, Boston, 1961, p. 501.
11. Report of the National Commission on Urban Problems to the Congress and to the President of the United States, *Building the American City*, 91st Congress, 1st Ses-

sion, House Document No. 91–34. Submitted to Congress and the President December 12, 1968, pp. 110, 111, 163.

12. McQuade, Walter, "Boston: What Can a Sick City Do?" in *Fortune*, June 1964, p. 135. Figures on New York land subsidies in Frieden, Bernard, "Policies for Rebuilding" in Wilson, James Q., ed., *Urban Renewal: The Record and the Controversy*, Massachusetts Institute of Technology Press (paperback), Cambridge, Mass., 1967, p. 609.

13. "Urban Renewal: A Policy Statement of the American Institute of Planners," American Institute of Planners *Journal*, November 1959, p. 220.

14. "Report on Your Profession," American Institute of Architects *Journal*, June 1960, p. 118, as cited in Blessing, Charles A., "The Architect and the Planner," American Institute of Architects *Journal*, March 1961, p. 86.

15. Blessing, *op. cit.*, p. 86.

16. *Ibid.*

17. Burchard and Bush-Brown, *op. cit.*, p. 502.

18. Rapkin, Chester, and Grigsby, William G., *Residential Renewal in the Urban Core.*, University of Pennsylvania Press, Philadelphia, 1960, p. 69.

19. *Ibid.*, p. 118.

20. Hickman, Leon E., "Alcoa Looks at Urban Redevelopment," address at the National Mortgage Banking Conference, February 17, 1964, Chicago. Cited in Bellusch, Jewel, and Hausknecht, Murray, *Urban Renewal: People, Politics and Planning*, Anchor Books (paperback),

New York, 1967, pp. 268, 269.

21. Anderson, Martin, *The Federal Bulldozer*, McGraw-Hill (paperback), New York, 1967, p. 221.

22. Greer, Scott, *Urban Renewal and American Cities*, Bobbs-Merrill (paperback), Indianapolis and New York, 1965, p. 61.

23. *Asphalt Institute Quarterly*, College Park, Maryland, January 1963, p. 3.

24. *Nation's Business*, Chamber of Commerce of the United States, Washington, D.C., April 1970, p. 41.

25. *Fortune Directory*, 500 Largest U.S. Industrial Corporations 1968; also *The New York Times Magazine*, June 22, 1969, p. 70.

26. Lundberg, Ferdinand, *The Rich and the Superrich*, Bantam Books (paperback), New York, Toronto, London, 1968, p. 40.

27. Leavitt, Helen, *Superhighway—Superhoax*, Doubleday and Company, Garden City, New York, p. 11.

28. *Ibid.*, p. 36.

29. Lundberg, *op. cit.*, p. 40.

30. Mowbray, A. Q., *Road to Ruin*, J. B. Lippincott Co., New York, 1969, p. 27.

31. *Freeways in the Urban Setting: The Hersey Conference*, Automotive Safety Foundation, Washington, D.C., June 1962.

32. *Asphalt Institute Quarterly*, College Park, Maryland, October 1967, p. 2.

33. *Asphalt Institute Quarterly*, October 1964, p. 2.

34. The prayer was adopted from a blessing by the Reverend Raymond F. Wrenn at the Virginia Road Builders' Association banquet in 1965.

255

NOTES

Cited in Leavitt, *op. cit.*, pp. 115, 116.

35. Sources on pollution; *Time*, February 2, 1970, p. 59. Mowbray, *op. cit.*, p. 213.

36. Boston *Globe*, June 3, 1970, p. 2.

37. Williams, Harry A., *The Motor Vehicle in an Evolving Urban Society*. Address to the Fifth World Meeting, International Road Federation, September 20, 1966, Automobile Manufacturers Association, Inc., Detroit, Michigan, p. 5.

38. Mowbray, *op. cit.*, p. 11.

39. Cited in Campaglia, Muriel, "In the Path of the Interstates," *City* magazine, June/July 1970, pp. 28, 30.

40. *The New York Times*, July 13, 1970, p. 62.

41. Kendrick, Boyce, "The Bumpy Road to a Better Highway," American Institute of Architects *Journal*, February 1969, p. 70.

42. *City* magazine, November 1967, p. 16.

43. Gooding, Judson, "How Baltimore Tamed the Highway Monster," *Fortune*, February 1970, pp. 152, 157.

44. Massachusetts Institute of Technology, Urban Systems Laboratory, *The Impacts of Highways on Environmental Values*, Cambridge, Mass., March 1969, pp. 22, 23, 59, 62, 63.

45. *Freeways in the Urban Setting, op. cit.*

46. Moore, Charles W., "You Have to Pay for the Public Life," *Perspetca 9/10*, Yale architectural journal, 1965, p. 97.

47. *Constructor: The Management Magazine*, November 1967, p. 27; *Hearing Before the National Commission on Urban Problems*, Volume 4, September 1967, U.S. Government Printing Office, Washington, D.C., February 1968.

48. *Business Week*, December 6, 1969, p. 150.

49. Lessing, Lawrence, "Systems Engineering Invades the City," *Fortune*, January 1968, p. 221.

50. *Business Week*, op. cit., p. 144.

51. *Ibid.*

52. Kaplan, Samuel, "Bridging the Gap from Rhetoric to Reality: The New York State Urban Development Corporation," *Forum*, November 1969, p. 73.

53. Schickel, Richard, "New York's Mr. Urban Renewal," *The New York Times Magazine*, March 1, 1970, pp. 30–42.

54. *Ibid.*, p. 36.

55. Logue, Edward J., "Urban Ruin—or Urban Renewal?" *The New York Times Magazine*, November 9, 1958, p. 33.

56. Boston Redevelopment Authority, *Low Rent Housing in the South End: BRA Programs for Supplying Low Rent Housing Units in the South End Urban Renewal Area*, November 1966, cited in *Report on South End Urban Renewal Plan for Boston*, City Council Hearing, March 25, 1968, Urban Field Service (Harvard Graduate School of Design) and Urban Planning Aid (monograph), Cambridge, Mass., p. 16.

57. *Report on South End Urban Renewal Plan for Boston*, City Council Hearing, March 25, 1968, p. 16.

58. Marcuse, Herbert, *An Essay on Liberation*, Beacon Press (paperback), Boston, p. 33.

CHAPTER IV

1. American Institute of Architects *Journal*, August 1952, p. 74.
2. *The New York Times*, June 20, 1968, p. 1.
3. *Architectural Forum*, July–August 1968, p. 72.
4. *Architectural Forum*, April 1968, pp. 35–36.
5. In Millstein, Gilbert, and Falk, Sam, *New York: True North*, Doubleday and Co., New York, 1964, p. 168.
6. Romney, Hugh, "The Hog Farm," in *The Realist*, November–December 1969, No. 86, p. 28.
7. Burnham, Daniel H., *Report on the Improvement of Manila* (Chicago, 1905) and *Report on the Proposed Plan of the City of Baguio, Province of Benquet, Philippine Islands* (Chicago, 1905). Typewritten reports to the U.S. Secretary of War (mss. in the possession of Avery Memorial Library). Cited in Klare, Michael T., "The Architecture of Imperial America," *Science and Society*, Summer–Fall 1969, pp. 281–82.
8. Rebori, A. N., "The Works of William E. Parsons in the Philippine Islands," in *Architectural Record*, XL (May 1917), p. 434. Cited in Klare, *op. cit.*, p. 282.
9. Moynihan, Daniel P., "Architecture in a Time of Trouble," Press release at 1969 convention of the American Institute of Architects and the Royal Architecture Institute of Canada, Chicago, June 23, 1969.
10. *Ibid.*
11. Hitler, Adolf, *Mein Kampf*, Houghton Mifflin, Boston, 1943, p. 266.
12. Moynihan, *op. cit.*
13. Lane, Barbara M., *Architecture and Politics in Germany 1918–1945*, Harvard University Press, Cambridge, Mass., 1968.
14. *Ibid.*, p. 188.
15. Moynihan, *op. cit.*
16. Lane, *op. cit.*, pp. 213, 214.
17. Hitler, *op. cit.*, p. 264.
18. Press release from Christian Science News Service, Boston, statement by Araldo A. Cossutta, August 26, 1967.
19. Spreiregen, Paul D., for the American Institute of Architects, *Urban Design: The Architecture of Cities and Towns*, McGraw-Hill, New York, 1965, pp. 215, 216.
20. Committee on Civic Design, Boston Society of Architects, "The Architects' Plan for Boston" (mimeo), 1961, pp. 1, 3.
21. Spreiregen, *op. cit.*, p. 132.
22. *Ibid.*

CHAPTER V

1. Cobb, Charlie, "Whose Society Is This?" *New Republic*, December 18, 1965, pp. 13–15. Cited in Hayden, Tom, "Welfare Liberalism and Social Change," Gettleman, M. E., and Memelstein, D., editors, *The Great Society Reader*, Vintage (paperback), New York, 1967, p. 482.

NOTES

2. In Maximoff, G. E., *The Political Philosophy of Bakunin*, The Free Press of Glencoe, Collier-Macmillan (paperback), New York, 1953, p. 77.
3. *Architectural Forum*, September, 1968, p. 87.
4. American Institute of Architects, Hunt, William D., editor, *Comprehensive Architectural Services*, McGraw-Hill, New York, 1965, p. 97.
5. American Institute of Architects, *Your Chapter Guide to Effective Public Relations*, AIA brochure, 1735 New York Avenue, N.W., Washington, D.C., December 1968, p. 8.
6. *Ibid.*, p. 4.
7. Scheick, William H., "Rx for Growing Pains," American Institute of Architects *Journal*, July 1969, p. 35.
8. *ARA News*, newsletter of the Society of American Registered Architects, No. 13, September 1969, p. 3.
9. *Ibid.*
10. Scheick, *op. cit.*, p. 35.
11. Hoffman, Abbie, *Revolution for the Hell of It*, Dial (paperback), New York 1968, p. 187.
12. Scully, Vincent, Jr., "The Death of the Street," *Perspecta 8*, Yale architectural journal, 1963, p. 94.
13. Kahn, Louis I., address before the Boston Society of Architects, April 5, 1966, at the MIT Student Center, in the Boston Society of Architects *Journal*, No. 1, 1967, p. 14.
14. Miller, Naomi, book review in the *Journal* of the Society of Architectural Historians, December 1967, p. 319.
15. Norberg-Schulz, Christian, "Less or More?" *Architec-*
tural Review, April 1968, p. 257.
16. Venturi, Robert, *Complexity and Contradiction in Architecture*, the Museum of Modern Art (paperback), New York, 1966, p. 24.
17. *Ibid.*
18. *Ibid.*
19. *Ibid.*, p. 60.
20. *Ibid.*, p. 20. Quote is from Robert L. Geddes (an architect), in the Philadelphia *Evening Bulletin*, February 2, 1965, p. 40.
21. *Ibid.*, p. 66.
22. *Ibid.*, pp. 93, 94.
23. *Ibid.*, p. 51.
24. *Ibid.*, p. 52.
25. Venturi, Robert, and Brown, Denise Scott, "A Significance of A & P Parking or Learning from Las Vegas," *Architectural Forum*, March 1968, p. 38.
26. *Ibid.*, pp. 38, 39.
27. *Ibid.*, p. 91.
28. In Maximoff, G. E., *The Political Philosophy of Bakunin*, The Free Press of Glencoe, Collier-Macmillan (paperback), New York, 1953, p. 77.
29. Boston *Globe*, May 22, 1967, pp. 1, 13.
30. Hall, Edward T., *The Hidden Dimension*, Anchor Books, Doubleday and Co. (paperback), Garden City, New York, 1966, pp. 1, 2.
31. *Ibid.*, p. 52.
32. *Ibid.*, p. 111.
33. *Ibid.*, p. 164.
34. *Ibid.*, p. 174.
35. *Ibid.*, pp. 167–68.
36. *Ibid.*, p. 177.
37. *Ibid.*, p. 188.
38. *Ibid.*, pp. 172–73.
39. Venturi, "Complexity and Contradiction in Architecture," *op. cit.*, p. 133.
40. Hall, *op. cit.* p. 119.

CHAPTER VI

1. Pope, R. A., *Proceedings of the First National Conference on City Planning*, Washington, D.C., May 21–22, 1909, American Society of Planning Officials, Chicago, September 1967, p. 77.

2. Address to Business and Urban Affairs Conference by President Lyndon B. Johnson (delivered by John W. Macy, Jr.), Washington, D.C., May 20, 1966, in Birch, David L., *The Businessman and the City*, Harvard University Graduate School of Business Administration, Boston, 1967, p. 45.

3. Lubove, Roy, *The Progressives and the Slums*, University of Pittsburgh Press, 1962, p. 114. The following references are cited: Tenement House Committee of 1894, *Report*, pp. 536–45; *The New York Times*, December 11, 1894.

4. *Ibid.*, p. 113. Lubove cites the following references: *The New York Times*, February 24, 1896, p. 2; Grebler, Leo, *Housing Market Behavior in a Declining Area: Long-term Changes in Inventory and Utilization of Housing on New York's Lower East Side*, New York, 1953, p. 97.

5. *Ibid.*, p. 243.

6. Steffens, Lincoln, *The Shame of the Cities*, Hill and Wang, New York, 1904, p. 163.

7. For a further analysis of how city reform served business rather than the poor in the beginning of this century ("The Progressive Era"), see Hays, Samuel, "The Politics of Reform in Municipal Government on the Progressive Era," *Pacific Northwest Quarterly*, LV, October 1964, pp. 157–59.

8. Address by Munson A. Havens, *Proceedings of the First National Conference on City Planning*, Washington, D.C., 1909, p. 84. Reprint by the American Society of Planning Officials, Chicago, 1967, p. 84.

9. Morgenthau, Henry, *Proceedings, op. cit.*, p. 59.

10. In *Urban Development for Commerce and Industry* (pamphlet), The Joint Center for Urban Studies of the Massachusetts Institute of Technology and Harvard University (no date), p. 6. Report on a 1963 developers' conference held by the Joint Center for Urban Studies of the Massachusetts Institute of Technology and Harvard University.

11. Delafons, John, *Land-Use Control in the United States*, monograph, Joint Center for Urban Studies of the Massachusetts Institute of Technology and Harvard University, 1962, p. 15.

12. In Weismantel, William L., "A New Vision in Law: The City as an Artifact," in *Urban Life and Urban Form*, Hirsch, Walter Z., editor, Holt, Rinehart and Winston, Inc., New York, 1965, p. 45.

13. Coke, James G., "Antecedents of Local Planning," in *Principles and Practices of Urban Planning*, 4th ed., 1968, published for the Institute of

Training and Municipal Administration by the International City Managers Association, Washington, D.C., 1968, p. 24.

14. Cited in Coke, *op. cit.*, p. 24. Walker, Robert, "The Planning Function in Urban Government," Chicago, 1941, p. 60; see also *Urban Planning and Land Policies*, Vol. II of the Urbanism Committee to the National Resources Committee, Washington, D.C., U.S. Government Printing Office, 1939.

15. *The New York Times*, December 21, 1959; cited in Lubove, *op. cit.*, p. 27.

16. Delafons, *op. cit.*, p. 27.

17. Borough of Cresskill vs. Borough of Dumont, New Jersey Superior Court, 1953, as cited in Delafons, *op cit.*, 30–31.

18. Delafons, *op. cit.*, pp. 18–19.

19. For examples of the integration approach, see *The New York Times*, "Lawsuit to Challenge Suburban Zoning as Discriminatory Against the Poor," June 29, 1969, p. 39. See also reports of the President's Commission on Urban Problems, 1968, National Advisory Committee on Civil Disorders, 1968, especially pp. 21–29.

20. Advisory Committee on City Planning and Zoning of the U.S. Department of Commerce, *A Standard City Planning Enabling Act*, U.S. Government Printing Office, 1928.

21. *Ibid.*, p. 8.

22. *Ibid.*, p. 10.

23. Fuller, R. Buckminster, *Operating Manual for Spaceship Earth*, Southern Illinois University Press, Carbondale, Ill., 1969, pp. 132–33.

24. Tugwell, Rexford G., *The Fourth Power*, paper delivered in Washington, D.C., January 27, 1939, at a joint dinner of the American Institute of Planners and the American Planning and Civic Association. Paper published by the American Institute of Planners.

25. *Ibid.*, p. 31.

26. *Ibid.*, p. 26.

27. *Ibid.*, p. 31.

28. *Ibid.*, pp. 11–12.

29. *Ibid.*, pp. 16–17.

30. *Ibid.*, p. 17.

31. Bell, Daniel, *The End of Ideology*, Collier Books (paperback), New York, 1961, p. 121.

32. Kennedy, John F., Yale University commencement speech, *The New York Times*, June 12, 1962, p. 20; cited in Roszak, Theodore, *The Making of a Counter Culture*, Anchor Books (paperback), Garden City, N.Y., 1969, p. 11.

33. Address by Robert C. Weaver, Business and Urban Affairs Conference, Washington, D.C., May 1966, in Birch, David C., *The Businessman and the City*, Harvard Graduate School of Business Administration, Boston, 1967, p. 10.

34. McNamara, Robert S., *The Essence of Security*, Harper & Row, New York, 1968, pp. 109–10, cited in Roszak, *op. cit.*, p. 12.

35. Ridgeway, James, *The Closed Corporation*, Ballantine Books (paperback), New York, 1968, p. 171.

36. Moynihan, Daniel P., *Maximum Feasible Misunderstanding*, Community Action in the War on Poverty, The Free Press, New York, 1969, pp. 24, 25.

37. Letter to *The New Republic*, April 9, 1966, p. 30.
38. Moynihan, *Maximum Feasible Misunderstanding*, p. 23.
39. Boston *Globe*, December 10, 1968, p. 1.
40. *The New York Times*, October 17, 1968, p. 37.
41. Moynihan, Daniel P., Memorandum to President-elect Richard M. Nixon, January 3, 1969, in *The New York Times*, March 11, 1970, p. 30.
42. *The New York Times*, July 2, 1970, p. 24.
43. *Hard Times*, July 13–20, 1970, p. 2.
44. *The New York Times*, July 2, 1970, p. 24.
45. Moynihan, Daniel P., "Who Gets in the Army," *The New Republic*, November 5, 1966, p. 22.
46. Collins, John F., "Technology for the Urban Crisis," *Technology Review*, July–August 1968, Massachusetts Institute of Technology, Cambridge, Mass., p. 19.
47. *Boston Globe*, November 30, 1970, p. 3.
48. *Ibid.*
49. Collins, *op. cit.*, p. 20, 21.

Chapter VII

1. Gorz, André, *Strategy for Labor: A Radical Proposal*, Beacon Press (paperback), Boston, 1968.
2. *Ibid.*, p. 7.
3. *Ibid.*
4. See Turner, John, "The Squatter Settlement: Architecture That Works," *Architectural Design* (England), August 1968, pp. 355–60. Also Turner, John, "Dwelling Resources in South America," *Architectural Design* (England), August 1963 (entire issue).
5. *The New York Times*, April 24, 1970, p. 37.
6. *Ramparts*, August 1969.
7. Turnbull, Colin M., *Wayward Servants*, The Natural History Press, Garden City, New York, 1965, p. 107.
8. *Ibid.*, p. 106.
9. Marcuse, Herbert, *One Dimensional Man*, Beacon Press (paperback), Boston, 1964, pp. 4, 5.

PHOTO CREDITS

Page 53 Urban Planning Aid, Inc.

55 National Periodical Publications, Inc., © 1971

59 (*top*) Pete Kirlin/Three Cats Photos

59 (*bottom*) Rick Stafford/Three Cats Photos

67 Photograph by Jacob A. Riis, The Jacob A. Riis Collection, Museum of the City of New York

69 Photo by James Foote

73 Richard Swanson from Black Star

76 UPI photo by staff photographer Paul Gorman

77 James Pickerell from Black Star

78 (*top*) Courtesy of Hammacher Schlemmer

78 (*bottom*) UPI photo

85 National Periodical Publications, Inc., © 1971

100 Drawing is taken from *My Work*, © Le Corbusier 1960. All rights reserved by La Fondation Le Corbusier.

101 *The New York Times*

102 Rick Stafford/Three Cats Photos

103 Rick Stafford/Three Cats Photos

110 The Connecticut Department of Transportation

115 The Asphalt Institute

116 (*bottom*) Keystone View Company

118 UPI photo

119 Wide World Photos

132 St. Louis *Post-Dispatch*, Black Star

135 *The New York Times*

138 State Historical Society of Wisconsin

139 Courtesy, The Bostonian Society, Old State House

143 Wide World Photos

262

PHOTO CREDITS

Page 144 Paul Ludwig Troost, Architect. From *Neue Deutsche Baukunst* by Albert Speer. Berlin, Volk und Reich Verlag, 1941.

146 Ben Schnall, Photographer

147 Hugo Röttcher and Theodor Dierksmeier, Architects. From *Neue Deutsche Baukunst* by Albert Speer. Berlin, Volk und Reich Verlag, 1941.

152–53 From *Urban Design: The Architecture of Towns and Cities*, by Paul D. Spreiregen, copyright © 1965. Used with permission of McGraw-Hill Book Company.

155 Courtesy, *Artforum Magazine*

157 Courtesy, *Progressive Architecture*

170 George Pohl

179 Geoffrey Clements Photography

180 Reprinted from *Arcology: The City in the Image of Man*, by Paolo Soleri, copyright © 1969 by The Massachusetts Institute of Technology. By permission of The M.I.T. Press, Cambridge, Massachusetts.

181 National Periodical Publications, Inc., © 1971

190 Chicago Aerial Survey

203 UPI photo

205 UPI photo

212 Reprinted by permission of Parker Brothers

215 *The New York Times*

224 William Holland

229 William M. Saidel

234 Hans Harms

235 Hans Harms

240 In Colin M. Turnbull, *Wayward Servants* (drawing by Nicholas Amorosi)

241 Labelle Prussin

242 Beryl Sokoloff

244 (*both*) John F. C. Turner

245 John F. C. Turner

251 Hans Harms

INDEX